Bottles of Emerald for the Demon Queen

A Play in One Act

Z.M. Wise

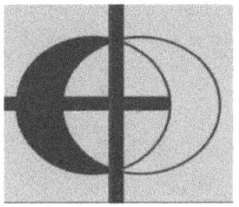

TRANSCENDENT ZERO PRESS
HOUSTON, TEXAS

ISBN-13: 978-1-946460-22-6
Library of Congress Control Number: 2019957278

Printed in the United States of America

Transcendent Zero Press
16429 El Camino Real Apt. #7
Houston, TX 77062

Cover design by Z.M. Wise

Bottles of Emerald for the Demon Queen

A Play in One Act

To the fallen victims of drunk and reckless driving, as well as their families and friends: my heart is with you, wherever you may reside. Pax vobiscum.

About Bottles of Emerald for the Demon Queen: A Necessary Disclaimer

This piece is based on a loose amalgamation of events. The play was written from December 15, 2018 to January 19, 2019. Keep in mind, Dear Readers and Viewers of the Imaginative Infinite, that a typical trial like this, though farfetched in nature, could potentially last much longer than a day. Believe me when I say that a session like this is highly unusual. If one had to narrow it down to a precise genre, one would place this play under 'alternative courtroom drama'. Although particular technical details may be skewed here and there, the direction is quite clear. I am well aware that the entirety of the trial is nothing short of unconventional, but then…that is the point, is it not? While it is never my intention to strike, offend, or attack, certain material may be considered offensive. Please understand that you have every right to feel offended, but it is still of your own accord. However, I will stand behind my work as a creator. That being said, I am whoever you portray me to be, as well as the piece you hold before you. You possess more power than I could ever imagine.

Namaste/Namago,

Z.M. Wise

Characters

• **Marcus Stewart:** Plaintiff and best friend of Robin West, the deceased victim in the case. Age: 29

• **Robin West:** Deceased victim of drunk driving (never seen onstage, only heard in audio recording and seen in photographs). Age: 29

• **Ana Fernandez:** Defendant and drunk driver who hit Robin and his brother. Age: 28

• **Salvatore West:** Younger brother of Robin West. He drove the vehicle during the time of the accident and suffered a broken jaw. Age: 25

• **Nick Fernandez:** Ana Fernandez's husband. He is a squirrelly human being, always nervous for some reason or another. Age: 27

• **Karina and Maximilian West:** Robin and Salvatore West's parents. Ages: 53 and 52

• **Honorable Amirah Sengupta:** The Judge presiding over the case. She can be described as unusual and unconventional at times. Age: 56.

• **Sandra Choi:** Attorney that the plaintiff and friend Marcus Stewart contacted. She is a fairly new trial lawyer, but she hopes that this will be the case to make or break her career. Age: 32

• **Jack Fredrickson:** Attorney that the court assigned to the defendant, Ana Fernandez. Age: 58

• **Daniella Kortokrax:** Witness who was present at the scene of the accident. Age: 22

• **Alastair Wiseman:** Witness who was present at the scene of the accident. He is a passionate poet, writer, and singer. Age: 29

• **Andre Villalobos**: Bailiff. Age: 36

• **Zeke Sanchez:** Court reporter. Age: 33

• **Tara Patton:** Jury foreperson (leader). Age: 40

• **Juror #8:** The only juror who stands up to Tara. Age/Gender: Left up to the Reader/Viewer.

• **Security Guard:** This particular guard works at the front of the courthouse. He plays an extremely important role in Scenes II and III. Age: Left up to the Reader/Viewer.

• **Various Jurors:** The other ten jurors are seen onstage, but they never speak. Ages: mixed

• **Officers #1 & #2:** Two police officers who guard the doors of the courtroom.

• **Various Courtroom Attendees:** Other than a couple court-room attendees who yell out during an uproar, these people fill the seats of the courtroom, anxiously watching the case unfold and end in ways that are beyond imaginable.

Synopses of Scenes

SCENE I
December 4, 2018. Skokie Court House. Skokie, Illinois. 8:30 A.M.-11:59 A.M.

SCENE II
December 4, 2018. Outside the Skokie Court House during recess and lunch. Skokie, Illinois. 12:00 P.M.-1:00 P.M.

SCENE III
December 4, 2018. Skokie Court House. Skokie, Illinois. 1:01 PM-5:00 P.M.

"Justice turns the scale, bringing to some learning through suffering." – Aeschylus

"Let us remember: one book, one pen, one child, and one teacher can change the world." – Malala Yousafzai

"There are you,
you drive like a demon
from station to station!" – David Bowie

"Dreams and reality are opposite. Action synthesizes them."
– Assata Shakur

"Demon Queen of Voodoo
sun in your vales of blue…" – Marc Bolan

"There's really no such thing as the 'voiceless'. There are only the deliberately silenced, or the preferably unheard."
– Arundhati Roy

"You're out of order! You're out of order! This whole trial's out of order!" – Al Pacino, *…And Justice for All*

"Gobernar es prever." – Spanish Proverb
Translation: *It is better to prevent than to cure.*

SCENE I

ROBIN WEST *and his brother* SALVATORE *were driving home on the night of November 28, 2018. All of a sudden, they were hit by one* ANA FERNANDEZ. ROBIN *was killed instantly, as he was sitting in the front passenger seat, also known as the most perilous seat in almost any vehicle, while* SALVATORE *merely suffered a broken jaw. The police recovered a bottle of 'Emerald Festival' absinthe. Since this brand of absinthe is illegal in the States,* ANA *is taken into custody. She has not a scratch on her, as she is found ranting, raving, and laughing maniacally. It is clear that she is in hysterics and cannot be reasoned with. She is barely coherent and speaks only in verse (both free verse and fixed verse).* DANIELLA KORTOKRAX *and* ALASTAIR WISEMAN, *two witnesses in different places on the road, see the entire tragedy.* SALVATORE *rushes home soon after being taken to the nearest hospital to be treated for his jaw. The parents,* KARINA *and* MAXIMILIAN, *break down. They hold a funeral a few days later. Upon finding out about the tragedy,* MARCUS STEWART, ROBIN'S *best friend, desires to take* MRS. FERNANDEZ *to court and make her pay for her actions, especially since the family is preoccupied with grieving. Before* MARCUS'S *vengeful mind and grief-stricken heart can take any legal action, the law itself immediately presses charges against her. The trial date is set for December 4. Everyone gathers at the Skokie Court House. The following people are present:* ROBIN WEST'S *parents,* SALVATORE, MARCUS, DANIELLA, ALASTAIR, NICK FERNANDEZ *(*ANA's *husband),* SANDRA CHOI *(plaintiff's attorney),* JACK FREDRICKSON *(defendant's attorney),* ANDRE VILLALOBOS *(bailiff),* ZEKE SANCHEZ *(court reporter), a private jury, and various courtroom attendees.* JUDGE AMIRAH SENGUPTA *enters soon after.* ANDRE *speaks.*

ANDRE: All rise! The Court of Skokie, Illinois is now in session, the Honorable Amirah Sengupta presiding!

Everyone in the courtroom rises. JUDGE AMIRAH SENGUPTA *walks towards her bench with a rather obvious look of disgust on her face. She sits.*

JUDGE SENGUPTA: You may be seated.

Everyone sits. There is a slight pause in THE JUDGE'S *voice, as if she does not know how to commence.*

JUDGE SENGUPTA: Forgive me, but after reading the police report on this particular case, I am not even sure where to begin. For a little over two decades, I have put away more pathetic, inebriated wastes of skin than the bottles they fused with in the first place. Never before have I come across such a case. Never before have I come across a story as gruesome, as demented, and as tear-jerking as this one.

She looks at the West family and at MARCUS.

JUDGE SENGUPTA: My sincerest condolences to you all. I, too, know how it feels to lose a loved one, to have that person's life slip away from you in the blink of an eye. It is a fleeting moment that one must eventually learn to let go. It is unspeakable, though, to lose a child no matter what the cause may be. Now, I cannot bring Robin back. I cannot guarantee a successful conclusion for those of you who are grieving. However, I *can* promise you one thing: you will witness the true power and might of the very definition of justice.

She looks at ANA. *Her voices switches from loving to ice cold.*

JUDGE SENGUPTA: There are so many sentences I could conjure up right now, but every single one of them would seal my fate as a judge in the worst ways imaginable. Instead, I shall tell you this: though it is against my profession and code of ethics to be biased on any issue, no matter what transpires here today, it is *not* going to turn out well for you. It will *not* lean in your favor. Do I make myself abundantly clear?

She breathes and looks at both attorneys.

JUDGE SENGUPTA: Counselors? You may proceed.

JACK FREDRICKSON *stands up, feeling quite confident that he will win this case even before it begins. He turns toward everyone and speaks.*

JACK: Your Honor, ladies and gentlemen of the jury, and all who are present in the court…I have two words for you: accidents happen. My client, Mrs. Fernandez, is the very living embodiment of that statement. Can we condone her actions, let alone her substance of choice? No. However, we can learn from her. She has promised never to touch a single drop for the rest of her life. I heard her whisper it to me many times through the mystical verse she speaks. Look at her! The poor woman is trembling! She feels guilty enough as it is! To be perfectly honest, this entire session is a waste of time. The West boy is under the ground. Even if the opposition wins, you will not solve the problem. The motives of drunk drivers will not be swayed or altered in any way, shape, or form. That is all.

JACK FREDRICKSON *sits. The jury looks rather shaken by* FREDRICKSON *and his unusually controversial and pessimistic opening statement.* SANDRA CHOI, MARCUS STEWART'S *attorney, stands up. Though she is still fairly new to her profession, she feels slightly confident. However, she still* seems *a tad nervous. She speaks.*

SANDRA: Judge Sengupta…er…Your Honor, members of the jury, and all who are present…it gives me no such pleasure to be here on this dreary December Tuesday morning. When Marcus Stewart, my client, thoroughly explained the situation upon inquiring about my services, I was flabbergasted, not only at this unnecessary tragedy, but at the fact that the victim's best friend decided to take the initiative instead of a family member. He then told me that the entire family was too preoccupied with grieving to think about such drastic action. I cannot speak for the rest of you, but that is one of the noblest gestures I have *ever* witnessed. In regards to Mr. Fredrickson's 'iconic two words', I would like to respond and double that amount. Yes, he is correct. Accidents happen, but do you know what I say? 'Accidents can be prevented'. Not all of them, of course. One cannot salvage every victim of an accident, but from a loss like this? It is inexcusable. If you remove two elements, none of us would be here conversing about this. Accidents…can…be… prevented, and I am here today to prove that fact.

SANDRA *sits. The court is mainly silent, but murmuring is heard in whispered echoes.*

JUDGE SENGUPTA: The counselors have delivered their opening statements. They shall now question the individuals they have brought with them to this trial. Before we commence these proceedings, I would like to warn every one of you. Some of these details are incredibly graphic and may become too intense for you. That being said, those of you who are not directly linked to this trial are free to exit these premises. As for the rest of you, this will be a fair trial. I will not tolerate any balderdash, outbursts, or humorous play. Does everyone understand?

Everyone nods.

JUDGE SENGUPTA: Very good. Counselors, you may proceed.

JACK *stands up.*

JACK: I would like to call a witness of the accident, Ms. Daniella Kortokrax, to the stand.

DANIELLA KORTOKRAX, *a tad nervous but also stoic, approaches the stand. She is wearing a business pantsuit and looks very professional. JUDGE SENGUPTA reaches down and pulls out an international anthology of love poetry, placing it atop her desk. She gives it to* ANDRE *and he holds it, beginning to speak. ANDRE tells her to place her left hand over it.*

ANDRE: Do you swear to tell—

JACK FREDRICKSON *interrupts.*

JACK: Your Honor, if I may, this is a tad ridiculous.

JUDGE SENGUPTA: *(Genuinely insulted)* And what is so ridiculous about it?

JACK: With all due respect, this book of…*(Holds the book towards his face)* love poetry from around the world does not make the following oath that convincing, now, does it? Don't you have a bible at the ready?

JUDGE SENGUPTA: Why does it matter what sort of tome she swears on, or *anyone*, for that matter? Besides, my court is run a bit differently than others. One might say it is… 'unconventional'.

JACK: *(Under his breath)* Clearly.

JUDGE SENGUPTA: What was that, Counselor?

JACK: Look, Your Honor…for a great many years, we have been using the Bible as the symbol of a binding oath, be it for marriage, direct religion, and making vows in a court of law. Now, please…with all due respect—

JUDGE SENGUPTA: *(Frustrated and irate, this is her last straw)* All right. That is enough, Counselor. You have made your point. Now, allow me to make mine. You keep saying 'with all due respect', yet the only thing you have displayed before me is an overabundance of *disrespec*t sans *any* regard for anyone's emotions, not to mention a prolonged session. Now, you listen to me like you have never listened to anyone before in your life. I have personally chosen not to use a bible or *any* book of holy texts because it has served as the catalyst that has led to countless wars. The Bible was also the device that was used against innocent astronauts almost a couple decades ago. Bart Sibrel was his name, I believe. This poor excuse of a human being approached…I am sorry…*harassed* these astronauts with a bible and attempted to coerce them into swearing that they never visited the Moon. Not to worry, though. Buzz Aldrin handed Sibrel his just desserts. *(She chuckles)* Nevertheless, I digress. This book of international love poetry symbolizes unity, diversity, and words so powerful that it forces you to be vulnerable for but a small minute, and that is beautiful. Besides, one does not require the attention of a deity, especially if they are a person of their own true word. However… *(Looks at DANIELLA and then the rest of the court)* if swearing before an almighty presence strengthens your oath, then by all means, feel free to do so. *(Looks back at JACK once more)* Now, then…now that our little 'chat' has reached its conclusion, can we let the bailiff carry out his duties?

JACK *nods, although he takes great restraint so as not to say a word.* THE JUDGE *looks at* ANDRE *and signals for him to continue.*

ANDRE: Place your left hand on the book and your right palm facing me. Then, place your left hand over your heart. Do you swear to tell the truth, the whole truth, and nothing but the truth?

DANIELLA: *(Follows* ANDRE'S *instructions)*: I do.

ANDRE: Then, we may proceed.

DANIELLA *sits.* JACK *gathers his notes and begins.*

JACK: Ms. Kortokrax, what is it that you do for a living?

DANIELLA: I am in the process of becoming an attorney. For now, I am an experienced paralegal.

JACK: I see. So, are you somewhat familiar with this process?

DANIELLA: I suppose. After all, I *did* watch *...And Justice for All.* Of course, I am familiar with this process. What do *you* think?

JACK: A simply yes or no will do.

DANIELLA: *(Scoffs)* Yes…

JACK: Were you working on that fateful night?

DANIELLA: *(Becoming increasingly sarcastic)* Yes. I had to work late that evening. It happens sometimes. You really hit the nail right on the head…

JACK: Do I detect a hint of sarcasm, young woman?

DANIELLA: Perhaps, but I figured that that kind of behavior was tolerated, considering the actions you exhibited prior to my questioning.

JACK *clears his throat, slightly embarrassed that his hypocrisy is coming to life.*

DANIELLA: Look, why don't I save you some time. Let us get to the meat and potatoes of why I am here. Ask me.

JACK: Very well, Ms. Kortokrax. Where were you on the night of—?

DANIELLA: I saw some poor soul in a vehicle die instantly at the hands of another vehicle.

JACK: I see. Would you care to elaborate?

DANIELLA: My pleasure. I was driving two vehicles away from the West brothers on the highway. As we approached the nearby exit…Exit 8, if my memory serves me, from out of no-where, this elderly Pontiac Bonneville sped toward us…thinking that the exit was an entrance. It drove from side to side, constantly swerving until it smashed into the right side of the West's vehicle. I imagine Robin died on impact, but Salvatore, the brother, was left with this twirling car. He did everything in his power to stop the now-totaled vehicle.

JACK: Yes? Do continue.

DANIELLA: I pulled over and rushed to the aid of Salvatore, whose jaw was broken and was crying hysterically. Before I could even take out my cellular telephone to notify the police and ambulance, they all arrived at once, almost as if someone else had made the call first.

JACK: Indeed. Concerning Mrs. Fernandez, what was your first impression of her?

DANIELLA: Upon seeing her, my initial reaction was that I thought she was a certifiable lunatic. The way she was laughing maniacally still haunts me to this day.

JACK: What did she say to you…if she said anything at all?

DANIELLA: Oh, she did, but it was nothing short of incomprehensible. I believe the most coherent statement I could make out was this:

"Ice women melt on the pinnacle of springtime hills.
Helios emanates mirages for the heated phase.
Killing for thrills,
setting songs ablaze.
Dawn's specters rise in morning chills…
through the forbidden lovers' windows gaze."

JACK: Ah, yes. That would be one of Mrs. Fernandez's 'verse trances'. She has been in one ever since I met her. Her husband Nick claims that it comes and goes.

DANIELLA: *(Perplexed beyond all belief)* So…this is a normal occurrence for her? Are we just going to pretend that this is all right?

JACK: Never mind that. I have one final question: do you feel that this accident could have… *(Looks at* SANDRA*)*…easily been prevented?

DANIELLA: *(Thinks for a moment)* There is no way of guaranteeing an individual's safety. I think this happened exactly when it needed to. I believe that nothing could have stopped it. Some things just occur.

JACK: *(Satisfied)* 'Some things just occur'. You heard it first-hand from Ms. Kortokrax.

JACK *walks back to his table, looking at* SANDRA *with an arrogant grin.*

JACK: Your witness, Counselor.

JACK *sits down.* SANDRA *gathers herself. After taking a deep breath, she approaches* DANIELLA KORTOKRAX.

SANDRA: Since all of the pertinent information has been revealed before the court, I only have one question for you: do you…love life?

DANIELLA: I beg your pardon?

SANDRA: It is a reasonable question. Do you genuinely love life? Do you love your life?

JACK: *(Standing up)* Objection! Your Honor, how does that question bare any relevance to this case?

DANIELLA *looks up at* THE JUDGE. THE JUDGE *speaks.*

JUDGE SENGUPTA: Overruled. *(Looks at* DANIELLA*)* You may answer the question.

DANIELLA: I love life very much, indeed. With all of my heart, I do. Some areas could use some improvement, but that goes for every person.

SANDRA: Indeed. Well, I have no further questions.

JUDGE SENGUPTA: If there are no further questions, the witness may step down.

DANIELLA *stands and walks back to her seat. On the way, she notices* JACK *smiling, quite satisfied with himself.*

DANIELLA: Don't you dare take my final statement to heart. I am on neither your side nor the side of the opposition. I am in this for me. Do you understand?

JACK *nods and Daniella sits. The court is silent for a brief moment.* THE JUDGE *speaks.*

JUDGE SENGUPTA: Counselors, you may call your next witness.

SANDRA: *(Standing again after being seated)* I would like to call Alastair Wiseman to the stand.

ALASTAIR *walks toward the stand. His long hair is tied back and he dons an all-black suit. Everyone is either weirded out or spooked by his appearance. He steps before* ANDRE.

ANDRE: Place your left hand on the book and your right palm facing me. Then, place your left hand over your heart. Do you swear to tell the truth, the whole truth, and nothing but the truth?

ALASTAIR: I do.

ANDRE: Then, let us proceed.

ALASTAIR *sits.* SANDRA *begins questioning him.*

SANDRA: Mr. Wiseman, what is your calling in this life?

ALASTAIR: First of all, I love the wording in your question. Secondly, I am heavily involved in the arts, whether it is in the Village of Skokie, the City of Chicago, the State of Illinois, or around the blue-green sphere.

SANDRA: I see. You are heavily involved in the arts in what way, exactly? Please elaborate.

ALASTAIR: I am heavily involved in a multitude of ways. However, I do have a full time position during the day that allows me to live comfortably. As for my direct involvement in the arts, I write, sing, draw/sketch on occasion, edit, publish, host, and promote.

SANDRA: Fascinating. You sound so passionate about your craft.

ALASTAIR: Indeed, I am. It is a lustful craving, a primal desire that never ceases to be.

SANDRA: I can tell. Please explain to me…what do you write, exactly?

ALASTAIR: Oh, almost anything you can think of. I stopped writing fiction and short stories years ago. It became far too tedious. I write essays, short verse dramas, vignettes, musings, quips, quotes, and a one-act play, not to mention notes for a screenplay. However, poetry comes most natural to me. Sometimes, I turn my poems into songs and sing them, later recording them when I have mastered the melody.

SANDRA: Well, thank you for sharing that. Now then, how well did you know Robin West?

ALASTAIR: Not very well at all, I am afraid. As a matter of fact, I was closer with his partner, Darren. Robin had proposed to him a week before the accident. He did not have a ring at the time. They were going to tie the knot and I was supposed to be his best man. Repeating these syllables out loud makes me shiver in the most negative way possible.

SANDRA: I can understand that. And where is Darren right now, Mr. Wiseman?

ALASTAIR: He is at home with his family. He told me that a major part of him wanted to be present, but with the current physical and mental state of his being, he just could not bring himself to do so. Besides, he is still in a great deal of shock over his loss. Robin was his other half, you see. They had an eternity ahead of them and it was stripped away instantaneously.

SANDRA: Of course. Now, in order for me to complete my last question, I would like to show the court the following audio recording that Robin left for Darren just one day before the tragedy.

SANDRA *hooks up a voice recorder to a couple of speakers and silences the court. She presses 'play'.*

ROBIN (audio): Salutations, baby. It's me. I just wanted to tell you how much I love you and how much you mean to me. We have escalated so far in this lifetime, Darren, and one day…we will be married. That, I can promise you. You are one in a million and I could not ask for anything more. I never knew what the definition of love was until I met you, and you are the living embodiment of the word. …well, all cliché spouting aside, I have a colossal surprise for you tomorrow night. Here's to two and a half years of complete bliss. I love you.

The audio recording concludes. The courtroom is silent. JACK *rolls his eyes.* SANDRA *clears her throat.*

SANDRA: What was that colossal surprise, Mr. Wiseman?

ALASTAIR: *(Choked up)* Robin was going to propose properly this time. He and Salvatore were driving home from the finest jeweler in town.

SANDRA: Thank you. I realize this must be difficult for you.

ALASTAIR *nods. She steps down, walking to her table. She looks at* JACK *with a pair of Arctic cold eyes.*

SANDRA: Your witness.

JACK *is simply amused. He chuckles to himself as he approaches* ALASTAIR.

JACK: Mr. Wiseman, I would like to begin by asking you the following question: how familiar are you with absinthe?

ALASTAIR: In what regard, Sir? Its origins? Its properties? Its usage? Its pros and cons?

JACK: Just what you know will suffice.

ALASTAIR: Right, then. Well, many individuals have dubbed it the 'artist's drink', and rightly so. It has been known to influence and boost many an artist's career. Some have even been known to paint *with* absinthe. The artwork, writing, and music are just fascinating after the effects have taken them over. And unlike most types of absinthe, this particular brand causes the consumer to hallucinate, and that is a fraction of the reason why certain brands are not allowed in the U.S.A.

JACK: I see. And do you yourself have any… 'experience' with absinthe? Please note that I speak of the brand 'Emerald Festival', the brand of the drink that was recovered at the scene of the accident.

ALASTAIR: *(Feeling a tad hesitant, but then answers)* Twice, actually: once in my own home and then once while staying in a hotel with some fellow creators after the conclusion of a beat poetry festival. Since I am a lightweight…pardon me…*feath-erweight* in general, it took barely an entire glass before I fell under its translucent spell.

JACK: Do go on.

ALASTAIR: Well, I wanted complete and total isolation, especially since my dear friends and fellow creators began to transform into these odd-looking creatures. They had the bot-tom half of a scorpion, the top half of a human, and then the neck and head resembled that of a wolf. Call it a 'New Age Chimaera', if you will. They began to chase me until I locked myself in the closet. Just then, I heard a raucous splash.
It seemed that one of my friends had stripped down to his briefs and jumped in the fountain outside the hotel. The staff members were very close to calling the police, but my friends straightened them out, despite their state of visual false prophe-cies. Long story short, I slept in the closet.

JACK: *(Sarcastically)* Goodness. What a delightful little tale. Perhaps you would like to share with the court your other expe-riences with various substances. Tell us how their effects tie in with creation.

ALASTAIR: Well, I have been high four times and drunk thrice in my lifetime…and I intend to keep it that way.

JACK: Do you, now? Are you not a regular user?

SANDRA: *(Standing)* Objection! Your Honor, the usage of substances outside of absinthe bares absolutely no relevance!

JACK: *(Looking at* JUDGE SENGUPTA*)* Believe me, I am attempting to make a point.

JUDGE SENGUPTA: Then, I suggest you make it, Counsel-or, and make it with haste. *(Looks at* SANDRA*)* Overruled. We will proceed as normal.

JACK: So? Are you a regular user, Mr. Wiseman?

ALASTAIR: I beg your pardon, but is this a series of inquisitive nuggets of curiosity, or an interrogation? It certainly feels like the latter over the former at this point.

JACK: Just…answer the question. The Judge has instructed you to do so.

ALASTAIR: *(Sighing)* No. I am not a regular user. Other than the times I mentioned, I do not touch anything. Perhaps a glass of wine after writing a book or recording an album, but that is about it. And judging by your condescending tone, you have a rudimentary understanding about the benefits of certain substances.

JACK: *(Raising an eyebrow, feeling smug)* Oh? Benefits, you say? Please enlighten me.

ALASTAIR: There are countless medical benefits of cannabis. I have seen it in action. It has aided numerous people… *and* animals with physical and mental ailments. There is THC, which contains the 'high' element, and CBD, which has a more calming effect to take the edge off in regards to mental and physical pain. There are also numerous psychedelics that can assist in the cleansing of negative energy, as well as rid some users of PTSD. MDMA is notorious for having that effect.

JACK: How fascinating. I should point out, though, that you yourself said that you do not dabble with substances, which leads me to the conclusion that said substances are, in non-technical jargon, 'bad'. Wouldn't you agree?

SANDRA *stands up once more*

SANDRA: Objection! Your Honor, this is pure coercion!

JUDGE SENGUPTA: Sustained. You may continue.

SANDRA: Mr. Fredrickson is putting words in Mr. Wiseman's mouth. He should not feel the need to prolong such commentary.

ALASTAIR: No, no. I will answer the question.

JUDGE SENGUPTA: Are you sure? Mr. Wiseman, that is not required of you.

ALASTAIR: I am positive. *Someone* needs to attempt to put this troglodyte in his place. *(Looks at JACK)* I said I do not touch substances by choice. I care not if someone uses substances for recreational purposes, just as long as they are being as cautious as humanly possible. It is just not my idea of a fun activity that I would partake in when the mood strikes. Obviously, there are certain substances that can obliterate your life. I daren't even give those instruments of death a second thought. With the more natural substances, as long as they are ingested in the correct dosage without excessive use, they might even go so far as to *salvage* a life.

JACK: I see. I have one final question.

ALASTAIR: Of *course*, you do.

JACK: Would you indulge in absinthe again?

ALASTAIR: Absolutely not. Some artists seek inspiration from outside sources, including many of the aforementioned substances. Some even long for spiritual occurrences and sessions of self-enlightenment, so they undergo rituals involving one of these so-called 'drugs'. The bottom line is that they are not *all* bad, just as long as they are used within the safety of one's home or a decent public area…not on the road. That is why we are all in attendance today, is it not? Obviously, this girl proves that tall tale for us. I mean, what would possess this 'bad' miscreant of a human to consume an entire *bottle* of absinthe just moments before taking a pleasurable joyride?

The courtroom fills with an eerie silence.

JACK: Well, I am satisfied…for now. No further questions, Your Honor.

JACK *starts to walk back to his seat when he hears* ALASTAIR *call out to him.*

ALASTAIR: Ah, but I have a final question for you.

ALASTAIR *looks at* THE JUDGE.

ALASTAIR: Your Honor, permission to ask Mr. Fredrickson a question.

JUDGE SENGUPTA: Is it at all relevant to the case?

ALASTAIR: Yes, Your Honor. In fact, you might find it to be very informative and could dismiss some of the obvious confusion.

JUDGE SENGUPTA: I will allow it, then. Permission granted.

ALASTAIR: Mr. Fredrickson, what on Earth are 'verse trances'?

JACK: Excuse me?

ALASTAIR: You stated earlier that Mrs. Fernandez enters these 'verse trances' where she only speaks in verse. Well, what in the blazes are they?

JACK: Young man, my client's issues with her speech are none of your concern.

ALASTAIR: Normally, I would feel inclined to agree with you, but since you made the term public and we all witnessed one of her 'poetic spasms' through recollection, I believe I speak for the entire courtroom when I say that we are all entitled to an explanation. The witness, Daniella, even pointed it out. So, why don't you just answer my question?

JACK: Very well. It seems that traces of the absinthe are still in her system and Mrs. Fernandez is not *fully* recovered yet, but when she is on the stand, she may come out of her 'magic spell'.

ALASTAIR: Thank you for that. Well, *I* am satisfied.

ALASTAIR *walks away from the stand and towards his seat, but as he passes* JACK, *they lock eyes and* JACK *whispers.*

JACK: You creative types are all the same. Outside of your nonsensical doggerel, you haven't even a tenuous grasp on reality and what life contains. You have *no* respect for your elders, either.

ALASTAIR: You know, it is quite a shame. I have genuine interest in the law and how it varies from state to state, country to country, and its many attitudes. Since you judged *me* falsely, allow me to perform the same action. You think that just because of the way I dress and carry myself means that I do not know the 'routines of life'. Is that what you think? Wrong, Sir. You are dead wrong. Besides, I have 'verse trances', too. It is when I feel I have channeled another presence and I cannot feel the pen moving as I create. The global community of the arts is not as villainous as you perceive us to be. You, though, Mr. Fredrickson…you wear your soul on your wallet, eagerly waiting for the two-dimensional green dead men to march to the inside of that brown leather. And as far as respecting my elders, most of my friends are twenty to forty years my senior, and it is because of people like you who influence my generation to rebel. How awful it must be to live a day in the life of you.

ALASTAIR *walks away quite satisfied.* ANA *giggles at the situation.*

JUDGE SENGUPTA: Will the counselors call their next witness?

JACK *stands.*

JACK: I would like to call Nick Fernandez to the stand.

A loud sighing is heard. NICK *stands up, nervous and anxious. He gulps.* NICK *is a timid man who is unsure of himself. He walks and makes his way to the stand.* ANDRE *walks towards him and gives the same instructions as he did with the other two witnesses.*

ANDRE: Do you swear to tell the truth, the whole truth, and nothing but the truth?

NICK *is hesitant. He gulps, avoiding all eye contact with* ANDRE.

ANDRE: Mr. Fernandez? Sir?

NICK *stands, frozen with some kind of guilty terror.* THE JUDGE *speaks.*

JUDGE SENGUPTA: Mr. Fernandez? The bailiff has asked you a question. Now, please answer it.

After shivering a tad, NICK *looks behind him, staring directly into* JACK'S *eyes as if he is a child seeking assistance or a puppy seeking approval.* JACK *simply closes his eyes and nods. No one but* THE JUDGE *notices this interaction. She keeps silent about this for now.*

NICK: I do.

JUDGE SENGUPTA: Then, please take your place on the stand. *(Looks at* JACK*)* You may proceed, Counselor.

NICK *obeys.* JACK *steps forward.*

JACK: Not to worry, Mr. Fernandez. I will not keep you up here any longer than necessary.

NICK *nods.*

JACK: Now, then…where were you on the night of November 28, 2018?

NICK: *(Laughs nervously)*: Oh, right off the royal leap, I see. No…preliminary questions for me?

JACK: *(Gives a small grin)* Take your time, Sir. Breathe and just let the answer flow through you.

NICK: *(Taking a deep breath)* Well, I was at home…waiting for my wife to return.

JACK: See? That was not so difficult, was it?

NICK *shakes his head.*

JACK: Did you have any idea of where Mrs. Fernandez could be at the time of the accident?

NICK: Most likely out being as 'absinthe-minded' as she possibly could. *(Chuckles)*

No one laughs in response to the quip. NICK *starts to receive a number of nasty looks.*

JUDGE SENGUPTA: Allow me to intervene for a brief moment. Mr. Fernandez, do you realize how serious this case is? Someone has *died* in the process.

NICK *looks down, nodding.*

JUDGE SENGUPTA: So, why have you chosen *this* time to make such crude humor?

NICK: I was just lightening the mood…diffusing the tension.

JUDGE SENGUPTA: Right…well, this is not the atmosphere in which to do so. Leave wordplay to people like Mr. Wiseman. Is that understood?

NICK *nods.*

JUDGE SENGUPTA: I am going to require a more verbal answer than that.

NICK: Yes, Your Honor.

JUDGE SENGUPTA: That's better. Proceed, Mr. Fredrickson.

JACK: Thank you, Your Honor. Mr. Fernandez, how long have you two been married?

NICK: Four years.

JACK: Splendid. And during that time, have there been any domestic quarrels? Any squabbles?

NICK: Well…it is inevitable for couples, isn't it? They will begin to fight at one point or another. It is natural. The question is: can you handle them in a civilized manner?

JACK: Well spoken, Mr. Fernandez. Such a universal philosophy. So…*have* you been able to live by it?

NICK: Here and there at times, while during others, definitely not.

JACK: I understand. Mr. Fernandez, why are you answering these questions in a cryptic fashion?

NICK: Cryptic in what regard, Sir?

JACK: Cryptic in the sense that you are not giving me a single straight answer.

NICK: My sincerest apologies.

JACK: There's a good lad. For my final question: do you think your wife deserves another chance as a free woman?

NICK: Without a doubt, Mr. Fredrickson. Everyone deserves a second chance. My wife may not have been in her right mind when this unfortunate tragedy occurred, but I know she would never commit such an atrocity intentionally.

JACK: Thank you, Mr. Fernandez. I have no further questions.

JACK *passes* SANDRA *on the way to his seat.*

JACK: *(Politely)* Your witness, Ms. Choi.

SANDRA *raises an eyebrow, but thinks nothing of it. Why was* JACK *feigning etiquette now? She shakes her head, collecting her thoughts. As she stands up,* ANA *hisses at her. They lock eyes.*

ANA:
As the streets are paved with storybook silver,
he knows not how he killed her.

**As the roads are paved with guilt-ridden gold,
profits from a prophet from curios that he sold.**

SANDRA *feels goosebumps growing on her body. She shivers,
but collects herself. She approaches* NICK.

SANDRA: Mr. Fernandez, what is your official profession?

NICK: I work in the medical industry.

SANDRA: Oh? Doing *what,* exactly?

NICK: Transporting medical equipment, to be precise.

SANDRA: Interesting. And does this career in medical equipment transportation require a great deal of travel?

NICK: Oh, yes. It is mostly out of state, but there are times
when I travel overseas.

SANDRA: That sounds like an adventurous benefit of your
job, does it not?

NICK: *(Smiling a little, relaxing)* Yes. Yes, it is. A change of
scenery never hurts the soul.

SANDRA: *(Returning the smile for a brief second)* Oh? What
else is good for the soul? Please elaborate on that.

NICK: Well, where do I even begin? There is watching a
sunrise with your partner, a heated mug of tea with honey and
lemon, long walks in nature, yoga, meditation, and much more.

SANDRA: These are all very enlightening. Speaking of travel,
I have a question regarding the enhancement of one's own soul:

would you mind telling the court how your most recent venture to Amsterdam went?

NICK *switches from relaxed to frozen stiff once more.*

NICK: H-h-how did you know my job sent me to Amsterdam recently?

SANDRA: I am so glad you asked, Mr. Fernandez.

SANDRA *walks to her table to retrieve an item in a plastic bag.* ANA *looks at her again.*

ANA:
Liquid jewelry for all to violently drink!
The truth is closer than you think!
Seeing Oedipus Rex turn reptilian,
scaled creature multiplies into spawn of eight million.

SANDRA *shivers again.* ANA *can clearly see how she is frightening her and she loves the reaction, practically feeding off it.* SANDRA *reveals a bottle of absinthe.*

SANDRA: This was recovered at the scene of the accident. It is a bottle of 'Emerald Festival' absinthe. Do you recognize it?

NICK *looks at* JACK *nervously, who shakes his head.* SANDRA *notices the avoidance of eye contact, looks behind her to see* JACK, *and then back to* NICK. *She is suspicious, but does not want to risk speaking up for fear that it would make her look like an imbecile, not to mention public humiliation and the probability of her being disbarred.*

NICK: Um…no?

SANDRA: No? You don't sound so sure of yourself, Mr. Fernandez. Do you care to try that once more?

NICK: *(Gulps)* No. No, I do not.

SANDRA: I am still not convinced. Perhaps this will ease your mind about this arduous decision. You swore before a judge in a court of law…and you swore under oath. The penalties of breaking said oath are tremendous. So, I ask again…is 'no' your final and definitive answer?

NICK: All right. Yes, I recognize the absinthe.

SANDRA: You do…well, that changes the circumstances, does it not? Do you think we will be able to take you seriously for the remainder of the trial?

NICK: Of course, you will be able to.

SANDRA: Oh, will we? You make it sound as if you have been completely straight-laced the entire time. However, you have managed not only to make one of the most insulting quips at the most inappropriate time, but you were only one syllable away from lying under oath. Do you see Zeke down there? *(Points to ZEKE)* He is a court reporter. It is his job to type out *everything* that escapes our lips in shorthand. Now, I think he can do without the sketchy behavior. Do we understand each other?

NICK: Yes.

SANDRA: All right. Now then, *do* you confirm that you recognize the absinthe?

NICK: Yes, but what does that have anything to do with Am sterdam?

SANDRA: Oh? I thought you already knew, but since you asked another 'dynamite' question, allow me to enlighten you and the members of the court. I did my research on this particular brand of absinthe. What I discovered shocked me beyond all belief. When it concerned 'Emerald Festival', it was only available in a small town of Amsterdam. It is sold in a quaint little shop. The name escapes me at this time. I tried to see if one could purchase it online, but alas, I was unfortunate at attempting that feat. That is why I asked.

NICK: Ah, yes. Now, that I recall, I did bring eight bottles back.

SANDRA: I see. And what is so special about this brand of absinthe? What makes 'Emerald Festival' stand out from the rest? How does it reign supreme?

NICK: It causes hallucinations. It guarantees that the consumer will hallucinate.

SANDRA: That is correct. And do you realize that 'Emerald Festival' is illegal in this country?

NICK: Yes…

SANDRA: So, why did you smuggle it? What was the mindset concerning that little move of yours?

NICK: To be perfectly honest, I thought I would not be caught with it.

SANDRA: Tsk, tsk, tsk. Such a pity. What did Mrs. Fernandez think of it?

NICK: She loved it. Some of my friends tried it as well.

SANDRA: So, the absinthe displayed a chain of different reactions? Interesting. What was yours?

NICK: What was mine…?

SANDRA: Your reaction to the absinthe. Did you hallucinate?

NICK: *(Hesitant at first, then responds)*: I didn't try it.

SANDRA: You never touched a drop?

NICK: No.

SANDRA: Then, why smuggle eight entire bottles? I do not understand.

NICK: I was frightened, all right? You know how there is a class of people who are lightweights when concerning alcohol consumption? I exceed that by far. To borrow a word from Mr. Wiseman, I am a *featherweight*, a self-proclaimed featherweight. Forget the level of thujone in 'Emerald Festival'. Are you aware of the alcohol content? It skyrockets like no other.

SANDRA: Does it, now? I hadn't realized that. So, then why would give it to poor Ana?

ANA: *(Standing up)*
Platinum beauty soldier saving grace,
fallen from angelic grace, the
clouds awaken from some fog cousin spell.
Exposed to the earth, I give birth to the
soul in which the Druid Queen bathes
seaside upside down, cannot stop looking at

voyeuristic pleasures, incantations and
invisible treasures bite bullets in the mind's war.

NICK: I-I-I…it was a present for her. A souvenir.

SANDRA: A souvenir? Do you honestly expect me to believe that you would give an entire bottle of absinthe as a souvenir? Why not a fancy trinket or an antique?

NICK: *(Looking down, hesitating to speak)* I don't…I don't know. I am sorry, Ms. Choi. I am a little flustered right now.

SANDRA: We all are, Mr. Fernandez. However, that does not excuse you from the question at hand. Answer it…now.

NICK: All right. I wanted to see her reaction to the beverage. I wanted to see those effects come to life.

SANDRA: Oh? And did they, Mr. Fernandez? What were those effects?

NICK: Besides the verse trances, she described seeing various mythological creatures, prehistoric beasts, primordial demons, false goddesses, and Lovecraftian abominations. Other than those, I believe it would be best to have her tell you herself when she is on the stand.

SANDRA: Fair enough. *(Thinks for a moment)* I have one final question. If you did not give Ana the absinthe, do you think that we would not be in this courtroom today?

NICK: What are you implying, Ms. Choi? Are you insinuating that I did this with evil intentions?

SANDRA: Not necessarily. However, do you feel at least *par* *tially* responsible for the premature death of Robin West?

JACK: *(Standing up)* Objection! False accusations!

JUDGE SENGUPTA: Sustained.

JACK: *(With a voice of panic and anger)* Your Honor, Ms. Choi is backing Mr. Fernandez into a corner, bulldozing an answer out of him!

JUDGE SENGUPTA: I understand, Counselor. Thank you. I think I can handle it from here. *(Looks at SANDRA)* You are walking a fine line, Ms. Choi. There will be no more of this 'playing detective' rubbish.

SANDRA: I am quite sorry, Your Honor. It won't happen again.

JUDGE SENGUPTA: *(Nodding and looking at NICK)* You are not required to answer that question.

NICK *nods.*

SANDRA: In that case, I have no further questions. You may be seated.

As SANDRA *walks back to her seat and* NICK *starts toward his,* ANA *stands up yet again. As she expels this verse, she begins to convulse in a violent manner.*

ANA:
I am the worm of arousal,
penetrating the ghost apple
that only my half-life eyes can see.
Burst out of my wailing womb,

O' Banshee Baby, spawn of starvation,
Mama's horns strike again!
AAAAAAAAHHHH!!!

ANA *convulses and screams in a fit of rage. The entire court freezes to watch this spectacle in motion. People want to exit the courtroom, but they stay for fear of what* ANA *may do.*

JUDGE SENGUPTA: Bailiff, restrain her!

ANDRE *runs towards* ANA, *grabbing her hands and arms and places them behind her back. He is almost successful in this endeavor until she kicks* ANDRE *in the testicular area. She then jumps on* ANDRE *and pins him down, beating him mercilessly.*

JUDGE SENGUPTA: *(Panicking)* Officers! Remove Mrs. Fernandez from this courtroom at once!

As soon as ANA *sees the two officers coming towards her, she lets go of* ANDRE, *curling into a fetal position. She cries her heart out.*

ANA: *(Weeping)*
Be with me when the Sun stops shining!
Love me before the Moon stops rising.
Hang my tears before clouded curtains to
forge the signature of She who Makes Proud Storms!

The two officers take ANA *out of the courtroom with minimal struggle. The court starts chattering loudly.* ANDRE *stands up, realizing he only has a bloody nose.*

JUDGE SENGUPTA: *(Banging her gavel)* Order! I say, *ORDER!*

The courtroom becomes eerily silent.

JUDGE SENGUPTA: For the remainder of this trial, there will be no more outbursts or tomfoolery of any kind! We will now have an hour-long recess so that everyone may clear their minds and nourish themselves. Meanwhile, I will see how our maniacal rock star is faring. This court is temporarily dismissed! *(Bangs gavel)*

NICK *walks back to his seat and sits down in utter disbelief.* THE JUDGE *walks to* ANDRE *and tends to him.*

JUDGE SENGUPTA: Are you all right, bailiff?

ANDRE: Not until this is over, Judge. Not until justice shows its face.

JUDGE SENGUPTA: It will, bailiff. It most certainly will.

END SCENE.

SCENE II

For this entire scene, THE JUDGE *and* ANDRE, *the bailiff, are unseen. Everyone else is standing outside of the courtroom. By now, it is twelve in the afternoon. Several people are eating various vending machine snacks and fast food. Meanwhile,* MARCUS *is leaning against a tree and staring off into the distance. The West family approaches him, followed by* NICK. SANDRA *hears* JACK *talking to* NICK, *and then she approaches* MARCUS *to tell him what she witnessed.*

SALVATORE: Greetings, old friend.

They all embrace.

MARCUS: Afternoon to you all.

A slight pause. MARCUS *continues.*

MARCUS: Look…I never fully had the opportunity to express my condolences and tell you all how sorry I—

KARINA: *(Interrupting)* Don't. Please…don't. We know how much your friendship meant to one another. You two were practically brothers…aside from Salvatore, of course.

MARCUS: This is true. Still, though…

MAXIMILIAN: Still, nothing. Robin is gone. Nothing can take that away. No one can resurrect him. I won't rest easy until that…that *parasite* is rid of once and for all.

MARCUS: This is why we are here today. We are here to rectify this tragedy, not only avenging Robin's passing, but *every* victim's passing through the act of drunk driving…and perhaps *all* reckless automotive-related actions.

MAXIMILIAN: *(Starting to weep, but with anger)* Do *not* refer to my son as a victim. He was a person, for goodness sake. He had the world at his fingertips!

KARINA: Maximilian…honey, he didn't mean anything by it.

MAXIMILIAN: I'm sorry. This is just…how did Octavio Paz word it? "I am living at the center of a wound still fresh…"

MARCUS: I understand. *(Looks at* SALVATORE*)* How is your jaw, pal?

SALVATORE: It will heal in due time. My heart, on the other hand? That is another tale that shall be saved for the life after this one.

MARCUS *nods.*

MARCUS: Are you going to be all right up there on the stand?

SALVATORE: I will be fine. I just don't trust Ana's attorney. Something does not seem right about him.

MARCUS: I am not particularly fond of him, myself. However, if you give him straight answers, you should have nothing to fear…emphasis on the 'should'.

SALVATORE: Speaking of straight answers, can you give us one?

MARCUS: I will do my level best.

SALVATORE: …do you think we have a fighting chance of

winning this case?

MARCUS *thinks for a moment.*

MARCUS: I believe so, yes. My attorney, Sandra Choi, is quite dedicated to her work. I should know. I used to stay up late with her, quizzing her for the bar exam like a drill sergeant. She will do everything in her power to see this through. You heard her opening statement, did you not?

MAXIMILIAN: Yes, but words mean zilch. We want substantial evidence.

MARCUS: True…and you will have it. You will see for yourself. Trust me.

KARINA: We do, dear. We just feel more reassured hearing it from you.

Another moment of silence passes.

SALVATORE: Well, we are going to head back inside so that I can mentally prepare myself for what is coming.

MARCUS: Stay strong, man. I believe in you.

They all embrace one last time before the West family reenters the courthouse. Thirty seconds pass before a squirrelly NICK sneaks up behind MARCUS, tapping him on the shoulder.

MARCUS: *(Jumping and whipping his head around in a startled motion)* HOLY CRIPES! Oh. It's *you.* You have got some nerve approaching me, you know that?

NICK: Look…I just wanted to say how sorry I am for every thing.

MARCUS: I don't want your 'sorry' or your pity. I want you out of my sight. You are making me lose brain cells with each word that exits your voice.

NICK: I know, but…I'm still sorry.

MARCUS: Is that all?

NICK: No. I have also come to beg for mercy.

MARCUS: Excuse me? Did I hear that right?

NICK: You did. Please…call off the trial. Call it off! My wife did not mean to do this. I swear…on behalf of the both of us.

MARCUS: You know, I could march straight to Judge Sengupta's chambers and inform her of our little 'interaction'…if one could even call it that.

NICK: Please. You don't understand. Ana was not in her right mind. She barely ever is. She just…she just loves that absinthe.

MARCUS: If what you say is true, there are facilities that care for and treat people like her. However, I don't think that is the case here. I believe *you* coerced her into drinking it. There is something about her…a soul within her soul that longs to cry out for help. And you, with your constant nervous demeanor and mysterious attitude…you are to blame, and poor Ana is caught in the middle. You are abusing her somehow, but that does not matter at the present time, does it?

NICK: What…what are you saying?

MARCUS: I am saying that if I knew Ana in another life, I might feel more inclined to feel a smidgeon of sympathy for her. Oh, yes. I have encountered people like you before. Most of my friends are women and I have lost a few of them thanks to beasts like you.

NICK: …I have nothing to hide.

MARCUS: Oh, don't you? Look at yourself. A courthouse and its walls should not petrify the average human being, unless they are in the wrong. Are you?

NICK: I…well…no?

MARCUS: Too easy. While it was technically an accident, your wife showed no mercy towards my best friend. I am taking her down.

NICK: I am begging you…one last time.

MARCUS: *(Raising his voice in anger)*: You listen to me, you germ! I have every inclination to tell Judge Sengupta everything that transpired, but because I want to see this all the way through, I will forget this ever happened as soon as we conclude this 'discussion'. YOUR WIFE IS GOING DOWN, NICK! THIS IS FOR MY FRIEND, ROBIN…THE HUMAN BEING *SHE* KILLED! SHE IS GOING DOWN!

MARCUS *calms down, turning his back on* NICK.

MARCUS: I have nothing more to say to you. Leave me.

NICK *darts the other way.* MARCUS *sighs, slightly relieved.*

Two minutes pass before SANDRA *walks by, overhearing a*

conversation between JACK *and* NICK. *She stands behind a certain part of the building so that they cannot see her or make out her shadow.*

JACK: And then what happened?

NICK: It was as if he saw right through me. He knew exactly who I was as a person.

SANDRA *gasps. She takes out a voice recorder and begins to record, even if it results in her disbarment.*

JACK: And what kind of person are you, Nick?

NICK: Not the best, I admit.

JACK: So, you *did* do it. You *did* force her to drink it. Why?

NICK: She has a mouth on her, I have to keep her in line *somehow.* In addition, if she didn't drink, I would beat her… show her who's in charge.

SANDRA *gasps again.*

JACK: I don't get it, though. Why absinthe? Why 'Emerald Festival' in particular?

NICK: It's just a joy to watch her freak out at something only she can see. She provides more entertainment than any television show.

They both laugh hysterically.

JACK: You evil mastermind, you. I would have done the same.

NICK: You won't tell anyone, will you?

JACK: That depends…on my…how did that poet freak put it? 'Green dead men in between folds of leather'?

JACK *holds out his hand.* NICK *reaches in his pocket, pulls out $800 in cash, and gives it to* JACK. SANDRA *attempts to snap a photograph of the bribery she witnessed, but she is too late. Who would believe her? She stops recording.*

Two minutes later, she rushes over to where MARCUS *is standing to tell him the news.*

SANDRA: Hey, you.

MARCUS *turns around.*

MARCUS: Hey, you, yourself.

SANDRA: How are you holding up?

MARCUS: Other than a brief Twilight Zone encounter with Nick, I am quite numb.

SANDRA: You did? What happened?

MARCUS: He acted like a starving child who longed for a banquet. He asked me to call off the trial.

SANDRA: So, they were talking about *you. You* are the one…

MARCUS: What?!

SANDRA: I caught Jack and Nick in the middle of a powwow.

MARCUS: Really?! What were they talking about?!

SANDRA: I cannot reveal what I saw and heard, but Marcus? I think we may have already won.

MARCUS *is speechless. They embrace. While coming out of the embrace, they stare into each other's eyes.*

MARCUS: Thank you, my friend. You have no idea how much this means to me…and Robin.

SANDRA: Well…perhaps when this all gradually fades away, perhaps we could be more than friends.

MARCUS: Perhaps. Whether we win or not, I still owe you dinner for the laborious task of being my attorney.

SANDRA: We *will* win, Marcus. Have faith in the law.

MARCUS: I have faith in *you.* That is plenty for me.

They nod in agreement and smile a little.

SECURITY GUARD: Okay, people! The trial is about to resume! You may want to head back inside!

SANDRA *and* MARCUS *walk side by side towards the entrance, saying nothing. As they reenter the building, the security guard stops* SANDRA.

SECURITY GUARD: Can I please have a brief word with you, Ms. Choi?

SANDRA: Certainly. *(Looks at* MARCUS*)* I'll be in there shortly. Go ahead without me.

MARCUS *walks into the courtroom.*

SANDRA: Yes, Officer? You wanted to see me?

SECURITY GUARD: Yes, indeed! I was watching the security footage…the live feed, to be exact, when I saw you holding a voice recorder. That was *you*, correct?

SANDRA: *(Feeling more frightened than ever)* Yes…

SECURITY GUARD: You *do* know that recording someone without their permission, whether by audio or video device, is highly unethical and in most places, against the law, correct?

SANDRA: *(Practically choking on her words)*: Yes…yes, it is. I just—

SECURITY GUARD: I am not finished. While you were recording, I became curious to hear what you were recording, so I turned on the audio function, though it seems to be a tad fuzzy.

SANDRA: And…? What do you think?

SECURITY GUARD: Through the garbled fragments of audio, I heard just about everything. I even saw the bribe. I think the Judge would be very pleased to capture another criminal and disbar a lawyer, as well as the original killer.

SANDRA'S *jaw drops. She cannot believe her ears.*

SANDRA: I don't know what to say. Thank you…so much. You just might have saved us and guaranteed a win for the Face of Justice.

SANDRA *starts to walk towards the courtroom.* THE SECU-RITY GUARD *calls out to her.*

SECURITY GUARD: Ms. Choi? You might need this.

He hands her a DVD with the footage.

SANDRA: Thank you! How can I ever repay you?

SECURITY GUARD: Give the opposition…absolute hell.

END SCENE.

SCENE III

Everyone has returned to the courtroom. ANDRE *now has a Band-Aid on his nose and one piece of tissue in each of his nostrils. After getting situated, everyone freezes in shock when they see* ANA *being brought back into to the courtroom. Everyone can clearly see that she is in handcuffs. The same two officers who escorted her out accompany her.* THE JUDGE *enters.*

ANDRE: All rise!

Everyone rises.

JUDGE SENGUPTA: You may be seated.

Everyone sits. Like the beginning, THE JUDGE *pauses to clear her mind and seek her thoughts. Thinking that this is the perfect opportunity to speak up,* JACK *does exactly that.*

JACK: Your Honor?

JUDGE SENGUPTA: *(Sighs with annoyance)* What is it, Mr. Fredrickson?

JACK: Are the restraints that necessary?

JUDGE SENGUPTA: …did you see what she did to the bailiff?

JACK: How could I miss it? I am just saying that she seems to have calmed down. Perhaps we can remove them.

JUDGE SENGUPTA: Not another peep out of you, understand? Unless it is directly relevant to the case, I do not want to hear you speak.

JACK: If I may, this *is* directly related to the case. This is my client we are talking about here. She deserves to feel as comfortable as possible…even if this is a trial.

JUDGE SENGUPTA: I will decide how matters operate during this trial. Do you understand?

JACK: Yes, Your Honor.

JUDGE SENGUPTA: And furthermore, you never requested permission to speak.

JACK *nods.*

JUDGE SENGUPTA: I never thought I had to repeat myself, but after the malarkey I have witnessed here today, there will be *no more* of it. I don't know how I could make myself any clearer than that. There will be *no…more.* I can only tolerate so much. Any more nonsensical poppycock and the consequences will be more severe than you know. *(Pauses to breathe)* Now then, Counselors, you may proceed again.

SANDRA *stands.*

SANDRA: I call Salvatore West to the stand.

SALVATORE *slowly stands and walks to the stand.* ANDRE *holds the book out in front of* SALVATORE, *telling him to place his left hand over it.*

ANDRE: Do you swear to tell the truth, the whole truth, and nothing but the truth?

SALVATORE: I most certainly do.

ANDRE: Then, let us proceed.

SALVATORE *sits.* SANDRA *speaks.*

SANDRA: Mr. West, what was your last memory before…?

SALVATORE: Before *it* happened?

SANDRA: Yes.

SALVATORE: *(Clearing his throat, holding back tears)* Robin and I were laughing after I teased him about how Darren would react following his marriage proposal.

SANDRA: And then…what happened after that? What occurred?

SALVATORE: I thought that witness, Daniella, told everything to Mr. Fredrickson.

SANDRA: She did, but I want to hear it from you. I want to hear *your* words…*your* side of the story.

SALVATORE: I…I… *(Starts to shake, his PTSD taking over)*

SANDRA: It's all right, Mr. West. Take as much time as you need. We realize how much of a tragedy this loss is for you.

SALVATORE: *(Takes two deep breaths and then speaks)* No. No, I am all right. My PTSD briefly consumed me by means of a flashback. It comes and goes. Well, Ms. Choi, I barely remember a single thing because it all happened so fast…so… fast. One minute, Robin and I were sharing what would be our last laugh together, and the next I see this vehicle drive towards us as fast as lightning, its headlights starting out as playful panther eyes and ending up to be this blinding illumination of doom. It swayed from side to side. Clearly, the driver was inebriated beyond all measure. I mean, this car came from out of nowhere. It drove *up* the exit as if it was a point of entry. The windows were tinted, so I could not see who was behind the wheel. After doing my absolute best to avoid this lunatic, I heard a loud bang, followed by Robin's grunting, the cracking of his bones, and the squelching sound of his flesh. I had no time to think, for that collision sent us twirling. I needed to stop us from spinning before someone else hit us. Luckily, I did… and pulled over to the side, but not before breaking my jaw on impact. I staggered out of the car to catch my breath. Then, I saw Robin's lifeless body. It was now a disfigured, horrific… mess. He was barely recognizable at that point. His face…his *face.* Oh, my gosh…I can't…*(Gasps and breathes)* I wanted to call the police, but someone else already took the initiative. An ambulance followed close by. The sirens were raucous enough, but the ringing remains embedded in your skull when it happens to you…and when it is coming for you. I could barely speak because of the extraordinary amount of pain I was experiencing. I heard a muffled sound coming from within the drunk driver's car. It kept growing louder and louder. When the cops finally opened the door, *she* fell out of the vehicle, laughing hysterically. It was not so much a laugh as it was a psychotic cackle. It was nothing short of unnerving. When the officers and paramedics attempted to recover Robin, that pat of pity on the shoulder weighed down my heart so much, but not as much as when they said, "We are so sorry." Those words haunt me to this very day. That's…that's what happened…precisely what happened.

A moment of silence fills the courtroom.

SANDRA: Thank you. Thank you, Mr. West. I have nothing further to inquire.

SANDRA *walks past* JACK *on the way back to her seat.*

SANDRA: Your witness, Counselor.

JACK *walks toward the bench, looking straight at* SALVATORE.

JACK: I only have one question for you, Mr. West, and then you may step down. *(Clears his throat)* Did you love your brother at all?

Several gasps are heard throughout the courtroom. SALVATORE *rapidly stands up.*

SALVATORE: What?! YOU SON OF A—

JUDGE SENGUPTA: Mr. West, try to control yourself.

SALVATORE: DID YOU HEAR WHAT HE ASKED ME?! WHAT KIND OF A QUESTION IS *THAT*?!

JUDGE SENGUPTA: I did, but if you don't sit down immediately, I will have no choice but to cite you for contempt.

SALVATORE *reluctantly sits.*

JUDGE SENGUPTA: Thank you. Perhaps Mr. Fredrickson would care to elaborate on the context behind the question.

JACK: There is nothing to elaborate on, Your Honor. I just want to hear his answer.

ANA: *(Attempts to taunt* SALVATORE*)*
**Little Robin flies to the nest of the West,
dive bombs into the sky of glass.**

SALVATORE: *(Brushing off the taunts, ignoring her)* What do *you* think?

JACK: I think that the sooner you answer this question, the sooner you may return to your seat.

SALVATORE: *(With tears streaming down his face)* I loved him with all my heart.

JACK: Thank you. No further questions, Your Honor.

JUDGE SENGUPTA: You may be seated, Mr. West.

SALVATORE *walks back to his seat in a huff, feeling insulted.*

JUDGE SENGUPTA: Are there any more witnesses?

SANDRA & **JACK:** No, Your Honor.

JUDGE SENGUPTA: If there are no more witnesses, then we will proceed with the questioning of Marcus Stewart and Ana Fernandez, who have both agreed to take the stand. The plaintiff will be questioned first and the defendant will follow suit. Are we ready to move forward with this trial?

Everyone nods.

JUDGE SENGUPTA: Counselors?

SANDRA: *(Whispering to* MARCUS*)* Are you ready?

MARCUS: *(Whispers back)* Let's do this.

SANDRA *stands up.*

SANDRA: I call Marcus Stewart to the stand.

MARCUS *stands, walking towards* ANDRE *with the most stoicism he has ever exhibited.*

ANDRE: Place your left hand on the book and your right palm facing me. Then, place your left hand over your heart.

MARCUS *does so.*

ANDRE: Do you swear to tell the truth, the whole truth, and nothing but the truth?

MARCUS: *(Without hesitation)* Absolutely.

ANDRE: Then, let us proceed.

MARCUS *sits.* SANDRA begins to question him.

SANDRA: Mr. Stewart, how long did you know Robin West?

MARCUS: Twenty-one years.

SANDRA: What was Robin like as a person?

MARCUS: Well, during childhood, he was the adhesive that kept this 'triangle of friends' together. He brought out the sporty side out of me, if I ever had one. Like me, he believed in the unexplained. We shared such long and intellectual discussions about life and its many aspects.

SANDRA: And how close were the two of you during his last years?

MARCUS: He had a bit of substance abuse trouble along the way, but after meeting Darren, that spark influenced Robin to reappear on the brighter side of the field, where the sunrise is nothing less than perfect.

SANDRA: That is absolutely beautiful. Now, then…tell me about your last conversation with him.

MARCUS: Our last conversation…well, he invited me over for a cup of tea and a game of chess. He stated that he had monumental news. When I became situated at his place, he told me that he was going to propose to Darren. My jaw dropped. I leapt up to embrace him tighter than ever, and congratulated him on his good fortune. Furthermore, he wanted me to be his best man. Naturally, I obliged. Even though we spent hours together, it only felt like a few seconds. After I hugged him again and bade him goodnight, that was the last time I ever saw him.

SANDRA: When did this happen?

MARCUS: Eight nights before the tragedy.

SANDRA: And what were your initial feelings when you heard the news?

MARCUS: A multitude of emotions: sadness, rage, and vengeance, all blanketed by a stationary numbness.

SANDRA: I understand. Why have you chosen to step forward instead of Robin's parents?

MARCUS: Because if I lost *my* child, I think that I would be lacking the ability of flowing speech as well. My child, bereft of life, would cause me to shut out the rest of the world while I was grieving. That being said, Robin's parents are still in mourning and will be for quite some time. I did not want to put them through this entire ordeal.

SANDRA *nods.*

SANDRA: Well, we all appreciate your presence. The loss of a best friend, let alone anyone, is, as mentioned before, unspeakable.

MARCUS *nods.* SANDRA *pauses.*

JUDGE SENGUPTA: Ms. Choi, do you have any more questions for Mr. Stewart?

SANDRA: No, Your Honor.

JUDGE SENGUPTA: Then, you may be seated so that Mr. Fredrickson may question your client.

SANDRA *nods and returns to her seat.* ANA *notices MARCUS crying a little.*

ANA:
Look! He cries out tears of milk,
rejected by the Illusory Temptress of Silk.
He expels discontentment for the Red Sun Pharaohs,
wishing for expertise in the cards of Tarot.

RANDOM COURTROOM ATTENDEE: For the love of all that is beautiful, would someone please make her stop?!

JUDGE SENGUPTA *bangs her gavel.*

JUDGE SENGUPTA: Quiet down, back there!

The courtroom fills with silence. SANDRA *turns to face* JACK.

SANDRA: Your witness, Counselor.

JACK *walks toward* MARCUS *while* SANDRA *returns to her seat.*

JACK: Marcus…er, may I call you Marcus?

MARCUS: That all depends, now, doesn't it? May I call you Jack?

JACK: I would you prefer that you do not.

MARCUS: I see. Then, I would prefer that you address me as Mr. Stewart, like everyone else has so graciously done.

JACK: Why does the precise nomenclature matter to you?

MARCUS: First of all, you have managed to call virtually everyone by their last names, so I have no earthly idea why you have chosen to single *me* out. Secondly, we are not on a first name basis. You are not my friend. This is your *job*, so don't try to lull me into a false sense of security by donning the guise of an ally.

JACK: *(Clears throat)* Very well. Mr. Stewart, what do you hope to achieve by winning…*if* you win, of course?

SANDRA *stands.*

SANDRA: Objection!

JUDGE SENGUPTA: Sustained. *(Looks at* MARCUS*)* You need not respond.

MARCUS: Thank you, but…I will. Everyone needs to hear and absorb this. I aspire to raise awareness by scaring the living daylights out of future potential drunk drivers.

JACK: *(Inquiring in a skeptical manner)* Scare them *how*, exactly?

MARCUS: By any means necessary. Let us face it. Even though the penalties for driving under the influence, let alone the prospect of murdering someone in the process, are severe, there still remains that fraction of miscreants who choose to live up to the very definition of selfish: consume alcohol and assume the position of a driver. We already have enough to fret over when it concerns reckless drivers, whether they are texting, looking down in general, undergoing sleep deprivation, acting like good ol' speed demons──

JACK: Are you just about through, Mr. Stewart?

MARCUS: I wish! Where was I? Ah, yes. Certain people remain ignorant when it concerns the existence of a turn signal. Some act as if they are making love to their accelerator pedals, utilizing their toiletries, i.e. toothbrushes, makeup appliances, and razors. Certain police officers abuse their power by chasing no one…need I go on? Now, we cannot hold a wake for Robin and reveal the horror of the damage that was inflicted upon him, akin to what Mamie Till did when her son Emmett was tortured to death by monsters who possessed human bodies.

JACK: Hold on just a minute. Did you actually just attempt to manifest an analogy between Emmett Till's gruesome death and its injustice with this unfortunate accident? How dare you! What makes you think you even have any authority on the subject?

MARCUS: Please calm down, Mr. Fredrickson. Allow me to explain. While these two unnecessary tragedies cannot be compared, they do share one minor similarity: This trial and that wake are desperate reality checks. "This is what happens when *that* happens." Action and reaction, you see. Awareness must be made.

JACK: *(Not even phased)* And you think this trial would alter the mindsets of human beings who choose to partake in drinking, an activity that has been occurring for thousands of years? Mr. Stewart, do you think that your attempt in heroics is futile?

MARCUS: You misunderstand me. I care not if people choose to consume alcohol. That is their decision. However, when entering a death machine that weighs two to eight tons and it is the spirit of Dionysus that convinces them to—

JACK: I beg your pardon. The spirit of who?

MARCUS: Dionysus, the ancient Greek god of festivals, drinking, and wine. As I was saying, he convinces you to drive under his spell. That is where the term 'spirits' entered into the alcohol lexicon. When you drink, they say a spirit possesses you, hence the blackouts, showing another side, feeling out of sorts, vomiting, et cetera. Mythology aside, it is still no excuse to operate a vehicle. You are now putting other people's lives in danger. In this case, it was a particular brand of absinthe. And from the bottle, demons emerged as opposed to spirits. *She* was kept alive from the very same substance that ended my best friend's life. That is how most drunk drivers survive: by staying looser than a dead fish handshake. However, is the alcohol blamed for the accident? No. It is the person. Alcohol has been glamorized for goodness knows how long, and look at the constant number of deaths that result from that undeserved fame. To further elaborate on something that Alastair Wiseman brought up, these same cretins think that a natural substance like marijuana is perilous, but where are the increasingly high number of deaths, hmmm? I don't see those statistics any-where. Do you, Counselor? Now, should you ingest marijuana before driving? Depending on the user and the quantity, it is debatable, but alcohol? It is absolutely out of the question. Like Mr. Wiseman, I have indulged in substances a few times, but that is it.

ALASTAIR: Here, here!

MARCUS *grins a tad.*

JACK: It sounds like you have little faith in the users of auto-motive vehicles.

MARCUS: Nay. I have little faith in humanity itself, and that faith is greatly reduced when I see our species driving. It de-pends on the individual, I suppose.

JACK: How depressing…

MARCUS: It is just the honest to goodness truth, Mr. Fred-rickson.

JACK: Truth or not, why do you choose to verbally pulverize my client? You do not even know her as a person.

MARCUS: For one thing, she will most likely not remember what I am about to say, due to her 'Super Elated Fun Time Land' state of mind. Secondly, I may not know her as a human being, but I do know of her breed all too well. My dear friend's grandmother was killed by her 'kind'. Thank goodness that the driver has been removed from the gene pool as well.

JACK: If you have all of this pent up rage, I suggest channeling it into a more positive activity.

MARCUS: Speak for yourself. If I need advice, I will ask someone like Ms. Choi. To quote my late grandfather on unsolicited advice, "When I need toilet paper, you can come rolling in."

JACK: And on *that* note, I have nothing more. No further questions, Your Honor.

MARCUS: Oh, but I do. I have something to say to our 'star' of the day.

MARCUS *looks at* THE JUDGE.

MARCUS: Is that all right? May I please have your permission to do so?

JUDGE SENGUPTA: I will allow it. However, please make it as quick as possible.

MARCUS: Of course.

MARCUS *looks directly into* ANA'S *eyes*.

MARCUS: If I knew you in another life and the circumstances were completely different, perhaps we would have grown to be bosom companions, confidantes without secrets. However, that is not the case, now, is it? Driving under the influence is awful enough, but absinthe is a dissimilar creature. I am unable to express how I feel, but in words so plain, perhaps I can deliver this understatement: I do not like you. I take one gander at you, and I feel more nauseous than ever. You are not even a person. You are even lower than a primitive organism that no one wants to be near for all eternity. I am picturing numerous scenarios in my cranium and all of them involve you experiencing great pain. Unfortunately, I am not a demigod. I am an irate fellow of sound mind. I need not do anything, for it is Karma who will be paying you a surprise visit, not I.

JUDGE SENGUPTA: Pardon me, but are you threatening the defendant?

MARCUS: Not at all, Your Honor, We have all been on both sides of the Karma spectrum. It is not our place to say whether a person should live or die…legality aside, of course.

JUDGE SENGUPTA: Indeed. Have you concluded your proclamation, Mr. Stewart?

MARCUS: I have, Your Honor.

JUDGE SENGUPTA: Then, you may step down.

MARCUS *nods and stands up. While walking to his seat, he passes by* ANA. *He stops.*

MARCUS: (Whispering) I see you.

He sits down.

JUDGE SENGUPTA: I believe it is time to bring our 'main attraction' up to be questioned.

JACK *stands up.*

JACK: Ana Fernandez to the stand!

The two officers help ANA *stand up. They escort her to the stand.* ANDRE *keeps his distance.*

ANDRE: Do you swear to tell the truth, the whole—

ANA *starts laughing hysterically.* ANDRE *looks at* THE JUDGE *with a puzzled face.*

JUDGE SENGUPTA: Officers, please calm her down.

Before the officers can take action, ANA *stops laughing, looks at* ANDRE, *and nods her head in response to the question.*

ANDRE: I will take that as a yes. Officers, please help her sit down.

The officers lead a somewhat catatonic-looking ANA *to the bench.* JACK *begins to question her.*

JACK: Mrs. Fernandez, how are you feeling right now?

ANA *holds her handcuffed hands and arms out in front of her.*

ANA:
Chained from this sphere as
animalistic as cave painting beasts,
out of animation and in primal pursuits.

JACK: Certainly. I can understand the lack of comfortability. However, it is very necessary. Mrs. Fernandez, do you remember anything from the night of the accident? Any recollection whatsoever?

ANA:
The stars swayed in opposite direction,
Moonlight Madre laughing until
feline eyes met with mine.
Kissing metal sacrificial paw in hand,
vanquished under pressure.

JACK: Yes? Do go on. What else?

ANA:
Dancing fast,
moaning last,
exit prevalent past.

SANDRA *stands up.*

SANDRA: Objection! Nonsensical doggerel!

JUDGE SENGUPTA: Sustained. What is it, Counselor?

SANDRA: Your Honor, are we really going to sit here and pretend to think that Mr. Fredrickson can translate and interpret every line of verse that Mrs. Fernandez is spewing? We need something more tangible than that.

JACK: *(Turning around)* With all due respect, I have been working with her longer than you, Ms. Choi. I understand her more, which is more than I can say for you.

SANDRA *sits down without a word, though she takes great restraint in order for her to remain taciturn.*

JACK: Mrs. Fernandez, what do you remember from that ter rible night?

ANA:
Daughters of the Seed, the Tipa goddess,
appearing in my chambers as ghost children.
Spectral scarred spawn, spurring sadness.
Madness melancholy, I am no daydream believer.
Expletives shouted, lights blinding me…
Explosion shattered, tinted mirror, scent of damage.
Aromas of death on the bridges to metropolis.
Little boy asleep with his face in all four corners,
internal lipstick splash for final effect.
Little boy in tears, blood on the street sans peace frog.

JACK: What an illuminating description. You did not mean to cause anyone harm, did you, Mrs. Fernandez?

ANA:
Cherubic girls kiss their wings goodnight.
Fly freely along frail fairies in fields of flight.

JACK: Well, how sentimental. Before I let Ms. Choi take over, I have one final question: where would you rather be?

ANA:
Home of the wild native lands,
home of the African origin sands,
home with interconnecting lovers.

JACK: Very good. Well, *I* have nothing further.

JACK *walks to his table. He directs his attention to* SANDRA.

JACK: Your witness…and good luck…

SANDRA *gathers her notes, takes one last glance at them, and walks towards* ANA, *her heart raving more than ever.*

SANDRA: Mrs. Fernandez, what is your full name?

ANA:
The ones who cut the rope and signed
documents are made of contagious confetti.
Named me Ana Estefani Fernandez for
Honorable Matriarch, the adhesive
that keeps families together.

SANDRA: And what were you doing before deciding to take a pleasure cruise that night?

ANA:
Absent, absent,
we all fall upside down!

SANDRA: *(Puzzled)* I beg your pardon…absent?

ANA:
Absent, absent,
working to dissolve in absolutes!

SANDRA: *(Annoyed)* I am sorry. I cannot do this.

She paces to and fro thinking for a second. Then, she figures it out.

SANDRA: Oh, I get it! Absinthe! You were drinking absinthe prior to your reckless driving! And how did you feel after the consumption?

ANA:
The Green Fairy slit the throat of
her Blue Sister, unleashing an
ocean of blood, cerulean poison infecting our shores.

SANDRA: I don't...I-I-I can't...

JUDGE SENGUPTA: Are we all right, Ms. Choi?

SANDRA: My apologies, Your Honor. I was never instructed on how to deal with a defendant who speaks only in verse. They never taught me that particular task in law school.

JUDGE SENGUPTA: And you think my professors taught *me*? Proceed, Ms. Choi.

SANDRA: *(Clears her throat)* Very well. Mrs. Fernandez, did you...intentionally or unintentionally...kill Robin West?

JACK: *(Stands up)* OBJECTION!

JUDGE SENGUPTA: Sustained. Ms. Choi, you may want to reorient that question.

SANDRA: Of course. *(Pauses)* Mrs. Fernandez, *why* did you kill Robin West?

JACK: *(Stands up)* OBJECTION!

JUDGE SENGUPTA: Sustained. That is strike two, Ms. Choi. If you do not organize your thoughts and rearrange the wording in your questions, you will find yourself in a *very* sticky situation.

SANDRA: I apologize, Your Honor. *(Thinks for a moment)*

Mrs. Fernandez, how long have you been married to Nick Fernandez?

ANA:
Invisible rings worn since birth,
engraving silver parchment with love's legality.
Half of eight's infinity symbol flees the scene,
lying sideways to look into each other's
delirious eyes and continue the struggle.

SANDRA: So, four years, then. Do you believe Mr. Fernandez is your soul mate?

ANA:
Two fog-laden souls meet and do not mate.
Interests held high, bound for this life.
Beauty for truth, truth for one last
look at the spellbound Sun...

SANDRA: Lovely. In those four years, has Mr. Fernandez ever hurt you in any way?

ANA:
Sentient creature is now a perplexed puzzle.
Sentient creature can think for herself...
until her walls cave in on her tissued mind.

SANDRA: What I mean is...has he ever physically or emotionally abused you?

JACK: *(Stands up)* Objection! She should not have to answer that question!

JUDGE SENGUPTA: Overruled. I will allow it.

JACK: This has nothing to do with—

JUDGE SENGUPTA: I *said*...overruled! Sit down, Mr. Fredrickson!

JACK *sits, becoming more nervous by the minute.*

JUDGE SENGUPTA: You may proceed, Mrs. Fernandez.

ANA:
Twice a blow to the cranium,
twice a beating to the limbs beneath,
twice a whipping to the back on which I lay,
lest he removes his sword of flesh from its sheath.

People begin to gasp, filling the courtroom with murmurs.

SANDRA: I am terribly sorry, Mrs. Fernandez. Somehow, though, I cannot say that I am the least bit surprised. Did you choose to drink the absinthe?

ANA:
Words form like grounded clouds that
make sweet visitations to our mortal level.
Failing to see the sympathy of control,
the concern for courage reaches starlight.
First morning star turns his branded back.
Last morning star takes me for acceptance.
That was every drop I drank.
That was all I wrote.

SANDRA: Mrs. Fernandez...did your husband Nick Fernandez force you to drink the absinthe on this occasion and other occasions prior to this one?

ANA:
I…cannot sense words.
Words wrote me here.
Suspended animation, suspending me in midair.
Seconds before the end erases my third eye's existence.
Third eye's existence…cleansed and polished.
Goodbye to the phallic faces forcing fallacies out of me.

SANDRA: Mrs. Fernandez, did your husband force you to drink absinthe today before the trial began?

ANA'S *look of hypnosis fades away. She looks directly at* SANDRA *as if she wants to beg and plea for help, but she cannot. Tears begin to stream down her face.*

SANDRA: Mrs. Fernandez…?

ANA *is fully conscious now and begins to sob uncontrollably, realizing just how guilty she is.*

SANDRA: I believe I have everything I need. Officers, will you please take Mrs. Fernandez back to her seat? I think she has had enough.

The two officers help ANA *stand and walk her back to where she was sitting. She cannot stop weeping. A moment of silence occurs in the courtroom.* JACK *becomes extremely nervous. He fears that his cover is about to be blown.* THE JUDGE *speaks.*

JUDGE SENGUPTA: We have heard both sides question the four witnesses, the plaintiff, and defendant. Before we send the jury off to deliberate the case and decide on the final verdict, the counselors will make their closing statements. Mr. Fredrickson, you may speak first.

JACK: *(Standing up, clearing his throat)* Ladies and gentlemen of the jury, as the Judge has stated, you have all heard the facts from both sides. This entire case now rests squarely on your shoulders. Will you choose to side with the naiveté of Ms. Choi's verbal defense tactics and Hallmark sweetness, or will you side with me and let me show you where justice *truly* lies? Let Mrs. Fernandez be a free person. Let her reunite with Nick, her husband, and let them live in peace without disruption. My client has been, by far, the bravest person here today…even if she was in a certain state of mind that is considered unusual. Your choice against my client will not even make a minuscule hiccup in the system. People will continue to drink. People will continue to drive. People will still continue to partake in both activities…simultaneously. Focus on yourselves. Worry not about how we operate in these judicial walls. Let Ana Fernandez be. Leave this woman…alone.

JACK *sits.*

JUDGE SENGUPTA: Thank you. Ms. Choi?

SANDRA: Thank you, Your Honor. Members of the jury and all who are present in this courtroom, with all due respect, as the opposition has so graciously repeated throughout the course of this trial, Mr. Fredrickson knows nothing about the meaning of justice. He would not recognize justice if it materialized into a human being and greeted him in passing. While it is partly true that Mrs. Fernandez has been through enough, so has the family of Robin West, the best friend of *my* client. They have enough to grieve over and ponder on. Please do not let the words of lip service transform into sheer ignorance. If you fight with me and deal with Mrs. Fernandez the right and ethical way, you will be showing the village, the county, the city, the state, and possibly the country that you demand a change. It does not matter what state of mind she was in at the time. She still placed someone's life in danger and stole that life in the process. Her 'other side' does not justify her actions. Mark my words…if you let this issue slip from your fingers, Mr. Fredrickson's morbid foresight will come to fruition. Now is your chance to be a part of something greater than yourselves. I cannot cease every cause of unnecessary death. I will tackle them one at a time…starting with this one. Make future potential drunk drivers think twice before they act. Perhaps if revelations that are more conscientious take place, the world would be less grim than it already is. I thank you all.

SANDRA *sits. The jury is stunned.*

JUDGE SENGUPTA: Now that the counselors have made their closing statements, the jury will now exit the courtroom to deliberate.

As the jury walks to the room in which they deliberate, THE JUDGE *sighs and leans back.*

JUDGE SENGUPTA: Andre, have you ever witnessed anything like this before?

ANDRE: Not at all. Say, Judge, do you have a funny sensation within your mind that something greatly intense is about to happen?

JUDGE SENGUPTA: Every now and then. Why do you ask?

ANDRE: *(Shrugging his shoulders)* Oh, just wondering.

SANDRA *and* MARCUS *look at each other.* MARCUS *closes his eyes and nods.*

MARCUS: Now, Sandra. Now is the time.

SANDRA *nods, feeling a tad nervous, but also very excited at the fact that this trial will take quite a turn. She stands.*

SANDRA: Your Honor, may I approach the bench?

JUDGE SENGUPTA: You may.

JACK, *feeling slightly confused, stands and walks towards the bench as well.*

JUDGE SENGUPTA: What have you to present to me, Counselor?

SANDRA: With your permission, Your Honor, I would prefer to speak to you about this matter in private.

JUDGE SENGUPTA: Ms. Choi, I realize that this is one of your first court cases, but the laws remain the same and you must abide by them. I cannot just give you special treatment.

SANDRA: Your Honor, you do not understand. The information I have before me could change the very course of nature in this trial. …please…

THE JUDGE *thinks for a moment.*

JUDGE SENGUPTA: Very well. Follow me, Ms. Choi.

They walk to THE JUDGE'S *chambers. Meanwhile, the jury sits and deliberates.* TARA PATTON, *the jury foreperson, speaks.*

TARA: I cannot speak for the rest of you, but that was the most peculiar trial that I have ever observed.

The others nod and murmur in agreement.

TARA: Well, I think it is fairly obvious what the moral and *right* decision is, correct? We put away that cat-faced little cretin once and for all.

JUROR #8, *someone who has stayed silent and very observant, feels uneasy about* TARA'S *rising dictatorship and fears that she cannot see both sides of the story. They speak.*

JUROR #8: *Is* it really that obvious, though? What about the logical choice?

TARA: And what would that be?

JUROR #8: We grant her another chance at life. A fresh, new start, perhaps. You saw the look in her eyes when the plaintiff's attorney asked her if her husband abused her. She started to cry. There is obviously a piece missing and I don't think we should be so quick to jump to conclusions. Maybe being a free citizen is her chance to escape the clutches of her husband for good and live a life as the independent and complex woman she is.

TARA: You *cannot* be serious. Even if she was abused, she took a human life. She could have left that monster if he was how she described him.

JUROR #8: Careful with your words. It is not as easy as you may imagine. One cannot just simply 'leave' the clutches of an evil entity such as Nick. What if Mrs. Fernandez has no friends or family…or *any* kind of support system whatsoever?

TARA: What the heck is this, the Jodi Arias case? You seem like you have sympathetic feelings towards that…that *fiend*.

JUROR #8: Tell me, then, O' Fearless Leader: have you ever been abused in a relationship? Have you ever been physically or sexually assaulted by anyone?

TARA: How *dare* you ask me that!

JUROR #8: I am attempting to make a point if you will indulge me. Have you?

TARA: *(Quietly)* No.

JUROR #8: Beg your pardon? I am sorry. I could not hear you.

TARA: No. I have not.

JUROR #8: And I rest *my* case.

Silence fills the room. At the same time, THE JUDGE *and* SANDRA *are in* THE JUDGE'S *chambers.* SANDRA *paces back and forth.*

JUDGE SENGUPTA: All right, Ms. Choi. We are alone as per your request. What was so pressing that you needed to pull me away from the courtroom? And why on Earth are you so frantic?

SANDRA: I apologize, Your Honor. I am just trying to formulate the words in my head before I tell you aloud.

JUDGE SENGUPTA: Take a deep breath, Counselor, and just…tell me.

SANDRA: Very well. I…I think Nick Fernandez is the person who killed Robin West.

JUDGE SENGUPTA: …excuse me?

SANDRA: Yes. While it was Ana Fernandez who technically hit the vehicle and took the life of Robin, I believe that her husband coerced her into drinking the absinthe on the night of the accident. My client, Marcus, even mentioned that Nick might have had something to do with it.

JUDGE SENGUPTA: How is that possible? Mr. Stewart was badmouthing Ana. He wanted her *gone*.

SANDRA: Can you blame him, Your Honor? His best friend was taken from him in an instant. Anyway, I have another piece of critical information that might be useful.

JUDGE SENGUPTA: On *top* of what you just told me? What could it possibly be?

SANDRA: I believe that Mr. Fernandez and Mr. Fredrickson are in cahoots, working closely together.

JUDGE SENGUPTA: …what?! …WHAT?!

SANDRA: I know. It is still sinking in for me as well.

JUDGE SENGUPTA: No, no, no. Hold it, Counselor. How do you even known all of this? I need physical proof…sufficient evidence in order to take further action. For goodness sake, Ms. Choi…I will need more than outrageous theories and conjectures.

SANDRA *pulls out her voice recorder and the DVD (with audio footage).*

SANDRA: What if I told you that I have every speck of evi dence right here?

THE JUDGE *is speechless.*

SANDRA: Allow me.

She proceeds to place the DVD into the television that THE JUDGE *has kept in her chambers for such occasions.*

SANDRA: The security guard at the front handed this to me when he was watching the feed.

They both watch the footage, but the audio does not seem to be working for some reason.

JUDGE SENGUPTA: Mr. Fernandez and Mr. Fredrickson are conversing. That is all well and good, but what are they saying?

SANDRA: Oh! My apologies. I can take care of that minor detail.

SANDRA *switches on her voice recorder so that the audio is in synchronicity.*

NICK (audio): She has a mouth on her. I have to keep her in line somehow. In addition, if she didn't drink, I would beat her…show her who's in charge.

JUDGE SENGTUPTA: *(Whispers)* What on Earth…?

JACK (audio): *(Laughing)* You evil mastermind, you. I would have done the same.

NICK (audio): You won't tell anyone, will you?

They both watch the transaction of bribery take place.

JUDGE SENGUPTA: That's enough. That's *enough*! I cannot watch any more of this. I…I cannot *believe* this! And you recorded them. …do you understand the legal principle behind that?

SANDRA *switches off the television set after taking out the DVD.*

SANDRA: Yes, Your Honor. Normally, I would not go against my prior teachings, but for the sake of morality, I deemed it necessary. I apologize.

JUDGE SENGUPTA: *(Sighs)* No. No, I would have taken the same course of action.

A moment of silence passes.

SANDRA: You know, I had such concrete motives during my closing statement, even after questioning Mrs. Fernandez, but…but, now, I just don't know.

JUDGE SENGUPTA: And I condemned Mrs. Fernandez before the trial even began.

SANDRA: Well…what are we going to do, Your Honor? How can we right the wrongs? We cannot lock her up, *now.*

JUDGE SENGUPTA: Just a moment. Let me think.

Another minute of silence passes.

JUDGE SENGUPTA: All right. We have to separate them from each other. *He* is obviously the criminal. Poor Ana was the bait…and we took it. When I questioned Mr. Fernandez, I should have known. I did not trust my instincts. Ms. Choi, you and that security guard just might have saved this case…and possibly a life. However, I will have to confiscate your voice recorder.

SANDRA *nods and relinquishes the rights to her recorder, placing it on* THE JUDGE'S *desk.*

SANDRA: What about Mr. Fredrickson? Will he be disbarred?

JUDGE SENGUPTA: Without a doubt. And I say good riddance. He is nothing but a…a…I am not even sure if there is a word that is suitable for him.

SANDRA: And…and what about the jury?

JUDGE SENGUPTA: *(Eyes widening)* The jury…we have to call them back to their seats. We must move and do so with haste. Let's go.

THE JUDGE *takes her notes, the DVD, and the voice recorder. They walk briskly back to the courtroom.* SANDRA *returns to her table.*

MARCUS: Where were you? What on Earth happened?

SANDRA: You shall see. And, Marcus? You were right.

MARCUS: About what?

SANDRA: *(Smiles)* Shhh.

JUDGE SENGUPTA: Andre, I need you to do two things for me.

ANDRE: Of course, Judge. Are you all right? You look like you have seen a specter!

JUDGE SENGUPTA: Never mind that. First, when I give you the signal, I need you to motion to the two officers so they can arrest Nick Fernandez.

ANDRE: *(Taken aback)* What? Why?! Isn't his wife the convicted one? Isn't she the one at fault?

JUDGE SENGUPTA: *Allegedly* convicted, bailiff. She is innocent until proven guilty, and as twisted as this case is, she… as difficult as it is for me to admit, is innocent. We are changing our plans. We need to separate the Demon King from his Queen, who is more of a victim of involuntary servitude.

ANDRE: As you say, Judge. What is the other task?

JUDGE SENGUPTA: Call the jury back. The verdict must be made. Their services are no longer needed.

ANDRE: But, Judge…the verdict rests with them. They need more time to—

JUDGE SENGUPTA: For goodness sake, call them back! Call them back *now*!

ANDRE: Right away, Judge.

As ANDRE *powerwalks to fulfill his task, the jurors have concluded their debate.* TARA *is sitting down and* JUROR #8 *is right next to her.*

TARA: I am sorry. I was not thinking clearly. I was just so ready to end this and put the matter to bed. I wanted to see her locked up…and pay for her unforgivable actions.

JUROR #8: I understand. But, now you see that it is imperative to explore both sides of a trial. Both sides have merit. One must gather *all* facts before making the final verdict. You need to remove the assumption that *every* defendant deserves to be sentenced to a life of imprisonment or death. There is still a great fraction of human beings who are wrongfully convicted due to one reason or another. It is all right, Ms. Patton.

TARA: I do not understand. Why are you being so nice to me?

JUROR #8: Because you are like me. You are only human… nothing more, nothing less.

A brief moment of silence passes. ANDRE *opens the door.*

ANDRE: All right, everyone. The Judge needs you all to return to the courtroom immediately. Do you have your verdict?

TARA: We do.

ANDRE: Very good. You will present it to me when the Judge asks for it. I will then collect it and present it to the Judge.

They follow ANDRE *back to the courtroom and sit down, waiting in anticipation. Everyone in the courtroom is speaking in different tones. Some are worried and some are restless.* THE JUDGE *speaks.*

JUDGE SENGUPTA: Quiet down, now! Does the jury have their verdict?

TARA: *(Stands up)* We do, Your Honor.

JUDGE SENGUPTA: Please give it to the bailiff.

ANDRE *collects it and hands it to* THE JUDGE. *She reads it thoroughly. She stands, sighing in relief.*

JUDGE SENGUPTA: After looking through this verdict, it will make what I have to say much easier. Due to some recent information that I have received, it seems that Mrs. Fernandez is not who she appears to be…and neither are her husband and a particular attorney.

People start speaking to one another. THE JUDGE *bangs her gavel.*

JUDGE SENGUPTA: In these two decades of my legal career, I have made very few mistakes, but none like the maelstrom I created this morning. I sent Mrs. Fernandez to the doldrums before the case even birthed itself in this courtroom. If you all will direct your attention to the television screen, we have evidence…*newfound* evidence, mind you, that will turn the tables of this entire travesty.

ANDRE *takes the DVD and inserts it into the DVD player.* THE JUDGE *synchronizes the audio as* SANDRA *did before. Everyone watches closely. Some people gasp. The West family is stunned. Both* NICK *and* JACK *begin sweating profusely. The footage concludes.* JACK *interjects.*

JACK: *(Stands up)* Your-your-your Honor…that was not me in the video.

JUDGE SENGUPTA: I never even said it was you, now, did I, Counselor? Thank you, though, for pointing out such a trivial fact for the rest of us. Sit down. You are not getting away *that* easily.

JACK *sits without hesitation.*

JUDGE SENGUPTA: As I was saying, no one on the defendant's side is who they appear to be, Just about everyone has hidden behind masks of deceit, only to show their inner ugliness, their true revolting colors. As the audio and video footage clearly stated, Nick Fernandez coerced Ana Fernandez into consuming the absinthe on the night of the tragedy. Based on his wording, this was *not* an isolated incident. It turns out that Mr. Fernandez's nervousness and stammering persona has another side that only shows its face behind closed doors. Perhaps the future potential drunk drivers present could take note and cease such behavior. I apologize for my livid tone, but an abusive person who not only tortures his life partner like the sadistic ghoul he is, but also *lies* under oath cannot be overlooked. And the fact that a bribe with someone on the inside took place is beyond my level of comprehension. An exchange of secrets for hush money right outside a courthouse is just downright insulting and stands against everything that the law conveys. That being said, based on the verdict of the jury and my own verdict in this matter, we find the defendant, Ana Fernandez…

Everyone sits on the edge of their seats in suspense. There is a slight pause before THE JUDGE *speaks again.*

JUDGE SENGUPTA: …*not* guilty.

THE JUDGE *bangs her gavel twice. Courtroom attendees are outraged. They start to rebel.*

COURTROOM ATTENDEE #1: This is bull, man! Lock her up!

COURTROOM ATTENDEE #2: Yeah! Make that murderer pay! Make her pay!

THE JUDGE *bangs her gavel thrice.*

JUDGE SENGUPTA: Order! Order in this courtroom!

The yelling from courtroom attendees grows louder by the second. THE JUDGE *has had it. This is the straw that broke the camel's back.*

JUDGE SENGUPTA: I said, *ORDER*!

She bangs her gavel extra hard. People seem to keep still and silent.

JUDGE SENGUPTA: You want an explanation?! Well, here it is! Mrs. Fernandez's husband repeatedly abused her, physically *and* emotionally. This is the person who supposedly took a vow to love her in sickness and in health, but he has chosen to gradually drive her to the brink of madness by experiencing trauma time and time again. According to her background, she has *no* living relatives and no friends whatsoever. How could she make any friends when her own husband keeps her on a short leash *and* a choke collar? Therefore, the only logical and moral option at this point is to separate the two of them… permanently. I hereby send the defendant, Ana Fernandez, to Alden Northshore, a nearby rehabilitation center with a court-ordered psychologist, a music and art therapist, and two therapy animals to accompany her on this journey. Upon her leaving the facility, she will return to the courthouse to discuss further actions. As for Nick Fernandez…bailiff, would you do the honors?

ANDRE: My pleasure.

ANDRE *walks over to* NICK *while motioning to the two nearby officers.*

OFFICER #1: Mr. Fernandez, would you please stand up?

NICK: Why?

JUDGE SENGUPTA: Because the officer asked you to. More importantly, because I want you to.

NICK *stands.* OFFICER #1 *takes out his handcuffs, cuffing* NICK'S *hands together. He does not put up a fight of any kind. He stands in place, frozen solid.*

NICK: What...what is the meaning of this?! Are you placing me under arrest?!

OFFICER #1: You catch on quick!

OFFICER #2: You seem rather surprised.

JUDGE SENGUPTA: That is *exactly* what we are doing. You will be taken into custody and held in jail until a separate trial can be made for you and your unforgivable crimes against humanity and your *former* wife.

NICK: She's *still* my wife! You cannot do this to me!

JUDGE SENGUPTA: She is only your wife on paper, but not for long. You would be surprised what the State can do. She is obviously not your wife by anything else. It seems you know *nothing* about love...or marriage, for that matter. You only know how to use your body and mind as weapons against one who puts her complete faith and trust in you. No more, Mr. Fernandez. It's *over*. Officers, please remove this abusive snake... this scum of the earth from these premises and place him in a nice, relatively comfortable cell.

NICK: *(Crying hysterically)* This is not me! This is not who I am! Please! Please forgive me! I beg you! I BEG YOU!

OFFICERS #1 & #2 *take* NICK *out of the courtroom and hand him to two more officers who are waiting outside. They return to the courtroom shortly after.*

JUDGE SENGUPTA: As for you, Mrs. Fernandez, the two officers will escort you to the rehabilitation center when you are ready.

ANA *nods, weeping.*

JUDGE SENGUPTA: And as for *you*, Mr. Fredrickson, I need to see you in my chambers immediately so we can discuss your… 'future'. Oh, and do not attempt to exit the building. Remember who you are dealing with.

JACK *nods and stands, with* ANDRE *following directly behind him.*

JUDGE SENGUPTA: As for the rest of you, this court…is adjourned!

THE JUDGE *bangs her gavel twice.* SANDRA *and* MARCUS *embrace each other tightly.*

SANDRA: *(Whispering in his ear)* We did it!

MARCUS: Yes. Yes, we did.

The West family runs to embrace MARCUS *as well.*

MARCUS: Everyone, this is Sandra Choi, my dear friend and attorney.

Everyone shakes SANDRA'S *hand.*

KARINA: We are still in shock about the sudden change in this trial, but we appreciate you doing everything in your power to secure our victory.

SANDRA: That is my job, Mrs. West. My sincerest condolences to you all.

SALVATORE: Thank you. That means a great deal to us.

MAXIMILIAN: Yes. Thank you, Ms. Choi. Forgive the lack of speech, but we can only handle so much information at once.

SANDRA: I understand that all too well. Will you all please excuse me for a brief minute? I need to speak to the Judge.

SANDRA *walks towards* THE JUDGE *before she disappears with* JACK.

SANDRA: Your Honor!

THE JUDGE *turns around.*

JUDGE SENGUPTA: Yes, Ms. Choi?

SANDRA: Thank you…for teaching me about the true meaning of justice.

JUDGE SENGUPTA: And thank *you*…for *reminding* me of its true definition. You are on your way to becoming a fine attorney.

SANDRA: *(Smiling)* I sincerely hope so.

THE JUDGE *nods and exits with* JACK *and* ANDRE.

The West family is still conversing with MARCUS. SANDRA *returns to join the dialogue. All of a sudden,* MARCUS *hears a voice from behind calling his name.*

ANA: M-M-Marcus?

MARCUS *whips his head around.* ANA *is standing on her own with the two officers behind her. Despite her innocence, the West family cannot help but shoot daggers in her general direction.*

MARCUS: You…what is it? What do you want?

ANA *breaks into tears.*

ANA: I am so sorry about Robin. You have no idea how terrible I feel about this. I will never be able to forgive myself. And I am not asking for your forgiveness. I just want you to understand.

MARCUS: How…how are you able to speak so coherently?

ANA: While, Ms. Choi was questioning me, she…*found* me. I returned.

MARCUS: Well, nevertheless, you will need to learn to forgive yourself…and live with it. I thought I knew the meaning of hatred upon meeting you. After this, I stand corrected. You have a long road to recovery, Ana. You were never meant to be in this courtroom, and incidentally…

MARCUS *walks closer to* ANA *to embrace her. They both weep together, holding each other tightly.*

MARCUS: ...I forgive you. You will be abused no more. Trauma will *not* become you any further.

They end the embrace.

MARCUS: Unless the officers allow visitation rights, perhaps you and I could be friends when you return to society.

ANA: I...I would like that very much. I will see you then.

The officers escort ANA *out of the building. Both* SANDRA *and the West family are shocked.*

SANDRA: I cannot believe you did that.

SALVATORE: Seriously...why, man?

MARCUS: Given the circumstances, difficult as they may be, could *you* see yourselves harboring hate for her for the rest of your lives?

KARINA: Yes, but...she still killed our son. Nothing can change that.

MARCUS: Technically, yes. However, Ana was a marionette being operated under the strings of Nick Fernandez. *He* is the criminal.

A moment of silence passes between them.

MARCUS: I will see you all quite soon. In the meantime, I owe my attorney a meal of her choice. Remember...I am here for all of you. Sandra, shall we?

SANDRA *nods as she and* MARCUS *walk out of the court-house. When they reach the exit, they slowly begin to hold each other's hands. They smile at one another. The West family follows behind.*

MARCUS: Sandra, what *is* justice?

SANDRA: In this day and age, I could not give you a tangible answer, other than the dictionary definition. Beyond that, only a few scattered people truly know. What we witnessed today, Marcus…*that* was it, and I will continue to extend my hand to the poor souls like Ana Fernandez who need a voice to help them be heard. At the same time, I hope that potential drunk drivers in the future will think twice before pulling the stunt that our poor friend did. I wish to assist the abused and help them fully recover. Many of them are wrongfully convicted for one crime or another. You know this. As long as the innocent are spoken for, nothing can stop us, and I will tackle each major cause for unnecessary death…one by one. Even if Ana was not guilty, her actions took the life of another human being. That cannot go unnoticed.

MARCUS: Are you saying that…if Ana was not abused and she was merely peer pressured into drinking the absinthe, she would be locked away?

SANDRA: Exactly. She is a special case, though. That cretin Fredrickson was correct about one thing: we *can* learn a lot from Ana Fernandez. She teaches us not to jump to conclusions, to take a look at both sides no matter *how* much they may shake us. There will always be that one group of morons who will be reckless on the roads of peril, but she made us think otherwise. …however, that is just *my* opinion.

SANDRA *and* MARCUS *walk hand in hand to a nearby restaurant.*

CURTAIN.

Alternative/Original Ending

TARA *wins the debate while the jury deliberate.*
JUDGE SENGUPTA *ends up convicting* ANA *of vehicular homicide due to her drunk driving, a.k.a. DUI manslaughter with gross negligence, sentencing her to five years in prison and a $25,000 fine.* NICK, *being a potential co-conspirator (considering he forced her to drink the absinthe), is sentenced to five-eight years in prison, as well as a $25,000 fine.* THE JUDGE *sarcastically says that the 'happy couple' would be reunited in death and that this rude awakening served as a reminder for anyone who planned on drinking and driving in the near future. End all automotive inebriation!* MARCUS *walks away quite satisfied, his last line being, "Goodness. I guess justice does exist, after all." This is a 'the law is the law' sort of ending where no one is innocent. As one could tell, this ending, while seeming harsh, stayed true to the original tone of the play, which was written in a poisonous mixture of anger and frustration as a response to the alarming amount of tragic deaths caused by drunk (and all other reckless) drivers. The final ending not only seemed more ethical, but a tad more cohesive to the story itself. While the case is closed in the play, it leaves the case wide open for you, the Reader and Viewer. What would you convey if you were a part of that jury? As a witness on the stand, could you provide some sense of clarity for the rest of the court? How would you react as one of the attorneys? What sort of power would you yield in that courthouse as the Judge? If you were the defendant or plaintiff, what would be racing through your mind? I leave these questions and more up to you. After all, creation itself contains an endless river of possibilities.*

A Brief Word on
'The Verse Trances of Ana Fernandez'

The following poem I am including was written for a certain notebook a couple months ago, but it was attributed to the play in a great deal. As always, I am that annoying creator who will refuse to explain what every one of my manifestations mean, unless I *want* you to know what they mean from the very beginning. As the Reader, that is *your* job, you lucky person. The only thing I will say about this piece is that when you separate each stanza, they become the temporarily 'absinthe-minded' Ana Fernandez's lines in the play. What do they mean to you, as a whole and in its individual morsels? Enjoy, in its entirety, 'The Verse Trances of Ana Fernandez'.

The Verse Trances of Ana Fernandez

Ice women melt on the pinnacle of springtime hills.
Helios emanates mirages for the heated phase.
Killing for thrills,
setting songs ablaze.
Dawn's specters rise in morning chills…
through the forbidden lovers' windows gaze.

As the streets are paved with storybook silver,
he knows not how he killed her.
As the roads are paved with guilt-ridden gold,
profits from a prophet from curios that he sold.

Liquid jewelry for all to violently drink!
The truth is closer than you think!
Seeing Oedipus Rex turn reptilian,
scaled creature multiplies into spawn of eight million.

Platinum beauty soldier saving grace,
fallen from angelic grace, the
clouds awaken from some fog cousin spell.
Exposed to the earth, I give birth to the
soul in which the Druid Queen bathes
seaside upside down, cannot stop looking at
voyeuristic pleasures, incantations and
invisible treasures bite bullets in the mind's war.

I am the worm of arousal,
penetrating the ghost apple
that only my half-life eyes can see.
Burst out of my wailing womb,
O' Banshee Baby, spawn of starvation,
Mama's horns strike again!
Aaaaaaaaaaahhhhh….

Be with me when the Sun stops shining!
Love me before the Moon stops rising.
Hang my tears before clouded curtains to
forge the signature of She who Makes Proud Storms!
Little Robin flies to the nest of the West,
dive bombs into the sky of glass.

Look! He cries out tears of milk,
rejected by the Illusory Temptress of Silk.
He expels discontentment for the Red Sun Pharaohs,
wishing for expertise in the cards of Tarot.

Chained from this sphere as
animalistic as cave painting beasts,
our of animation and in primal pursuits.

The stars swayed in opposite direction,
Moonlight Madre laughing until
feline eyes met with mine.
Kissing metal sacrificial paw in hand,
vanquished under pressure.

Dancing fast,
moaning last,
exit prevalent past.

Daughters of the Seed, the Tipa goddess,
appearing in my chambers as ghost children.
Spectral scarred spawn, spurring sadness.
Madness melancholy, I am no daydream believer.
Expletives shouted, lights blinding me…
Explosion shattered, tinted mirror, scent of damage.
Aromas of death on the bridges to metropolis.

Little boy asleep with his face in all four corners,
internal lipstick splash for final effect.
Little boy in tears, blood on the street sans peace frog.

Cherubic girls kiss their wings goodnight.
Fly freely along frail fairies in fields of flight.

Home of the wild native lands,
home of the African origin sands,
home with interconnecting lovers.

The ones who cut the rope and signed
documents are made of contagious confetti.
Named me Ana Estefani Fernandez for
Honorable Matriarch, the adhesive that keeps families together.

Absent, absent,
we all fall upside down!

Absent, absent,
working to dissolve in absolutes!

The Green Fairy slit the throat of
her Blue Sister, unleashing an
ocean of blood, cerulean poison infecting our shores.

Invisible rings worn since birth,
engraving silver parchment with love's legality.
Half of eight's infinity symbol flees the scene,
lying sideways to look into each other's
delirious eyes and continue the struggle.

Two fog-laden souls meet and do not mate.
Interests held high, bound for this life.

Beauty for truth, truth for one last
look at the spellbound Sun…

Sentient creature is now a perplexed puzzle.
Sentient creature can think for herself…
until her walls cave in on her tissued mind.

Twice a blow to the cranium,
twice a beating to the limbs beneath,
twice a whipping to the back on which I lay,
lest he removes his sword of flesh from its sheath.

Words form like grounded clouds that
make sweet visitations to our mortal level.
Failing to see the sympathy of control,
the concern for courage reaches starlight.
First morning star turns his branded back.
Last morning star takes me for acceptance.
That was every drop I drank.
That was all I wrote.

I…cannot sense words.
Words wrote me here.
Suspended animation, suspending me in midair.
Seconds before the end erases my third eye's existence.
Third eye's existence…cleansed and polished.
Goodbye to the phallic faces forcing fallacies out of me.

December 31, 2018

About the Author

Z.M. Wise is a proud Illinois native from Chicago, poet, essayist, occasional playwright, seldom screenwriter, co-editor and arts activist, writing since his first steps as a child. He was selected to be a performer in the Word Around Town Tour in 2013, a Houston citywide tour. He is co-owner and co-editor of Transcendent Zero Press, an independent publishing house for poetry that produces an international quarterly journal known as Harbinger Asylum. The journal was nominated Best Poetry Journal in 2013 at the National Poetry Awards. He has published five books of poetry, including: *Take Me Back, Kingswood Clock!* (MavLit Press, 2013), *The Wandering Poet* (Transcendent Zero Press, 2014), *Wolf: An Epic & Other Poems* (Weasel Press, 2015), *Cuentos de Amor* (Red Ferret Press, 2015), and *Kosmish and the Horned Ones* (Weasel Press, 2018). His debut play, *Bottles of Emerald for the Demon Queen* (Transcendent Zero Press, 2019), *was released in December of* 2019. His sixth book of poetry will be published by Cherry House Press in the early months of 2020. Other than these books, his poems, lyrics, essays, and book reviews have been published in various journals, magazines, and anthologies. The motto that keeps him going: POETRY LIVES AND LONG LIVE THE ARTS! Mr. Wise will make sure to spread that message and the love of the arts, making sure it remains vibrant for the rest of his days and beyond. Besides poetry and other forms of writing, his other passions/interests include professional voice acting, singing/lyricism/songwriting, playing a few instruments, fitness, and reading.

Read more about Z.M. Wise and his work on his website!
https://zmwise.wixsite.com/zmwisethepoet

Haven't had enough Wise Words?
Twitter: @ZMWisePoet

You still want more?!
www.youtube.com/ZMthePoet